Inside Challenging

"Over the past cent
of books, tapes, CDs, L
are grieving... But most of them mimic outdated theories.
Grief is too important an emotion to be left in the hands of
those who just want to recycle old notions, unsupported by
the latest scientific data."

"We are all different in our responses to loss. What we
have called in the past "symptoms" are really descriptions,
which vary from person to person. It is actually a personal
collage of feelings."

"Our culture contributes to feelings of disenfranchise-
ment. It does not acknowledge the losses of some people
who are often deemed invisible or devalued as human be-
ings because they are not part of the mainstream..."

" I've witnessed the damage caused by the stringent struc-
tures our culture imposes upon the grief stricken. Often the
peace they are entitled to is violated. The excessive cost of fu-
nerals, with all of their requisite trappings, demonstrates
how people are often exploited at the most tragic time in
their lives."

"We can create better pathways for integrating losses and
finding meaning and motivating those who are grief stricken.
We must eliminate obstacles and enhance opportunities for
creative discovery and hope."

No one's death comes to pass without making some impression, and we inherit part of the liberated soul and become richer in humanness.

-Hermann Broch

Challenging the Landscape of Loss

Why what we've been told about grief doesn't help.

Terence P. Curley

Published by Paloma Publishing

Cover photo courtesy
NASA Jet Propulsion Laboratory
California Institute of Technology
Spitzer Space Telescope photo of spiral galaxy M81

K. Gordon (University of Arizona) & S. Willner (Harvard-Smithsonian Center for Astrophysics), N.A. Sharp (NOAO/AURA/NSF)

Published by Paloma Publishing
28 Allen Road, Swampscott, Massachusetts, 01907
781-592-7693
manageyourloss2@gmail.com

**Media and speaking inquiries and
one-on-one counseling**

The AdvocatesNE
Box 1286, Marblehead, Massachusetts, 01945
340-998-5715
advocatesne@gmail.com

www.manageyourloss.com

Library of Congress Cataloging in Publication Data
Curley, Terence P.
Challenging the Landscape of Loss
CIP: (pending)
ISBN-EAN 9781503279636

1st Edition, January, 2014

Content

DEDICATION

In loving memory of my mother

Eileen C. Curley

She taught us with the Latin phrase:

Quid hoc ad aeternitatem?

(What does this matter in light of eternity?)

Author's note

This book focuses on new revelations about how we grieve. It outlines the latest scientific research, and debunks old fashioned theories about the process of grief, which can often cause confusion to those who are grieving. It also addresses the psychology of loss and explores the social context of related rituals.

I've witnessed the damage caused by the stringent structures our culture imposes upon the grief stricken. Often the peace they are entitled to is violated. The excessive cost of funerals, with all of their requisite trappings, demonstrates how people are often exploited at the most tragic time in their lives.

One of my professors in graduate school stressed the need for social justice in pastoral care. I never fully understood what this meant in being with the bereaved. Now, my eyes have opened as I perceive the unnecessary demands placed upon society's most vulnerable. This book lays the foundation for understanding that many current practices are poor science, and do not reflect spiritual principles.

We who truly want to heal ourselves or be caregivers to the bereaved must be in the forefront. We should be leading the charge to change the way society imposes commercially driven customs, often at the expense of providing the care and empathy the broken-hearted need.

Too many instances of catastrophes have devastated families and communities.

Now, more than ever, in the aftermath of both natural

and man made disasters we need to establish new pathways for meaning and hope in our lives.

Recent events, such as the typhoon in the Phillipines, gun violence in Sandy Hook Connecticut and the Boston Marathon bombings, have helped communities come together in grief and find the will to rebuild.

But so much more needs to be done.

We must rewrite some of the outdated scripts about how we help others at painful times. We must acknowledge the resilient spirit of grief as both a gift, and an empowering.

We can create better pathways for integrating loss, finding meaning and motivating those who are grief stricken. We must eliminate obstacles and enhance opportunities for creative discovery and hope for those who experience loss.

Researching and writing this book has broadened my vision. I hope you will find it enlightening and useful as well.

Terence P. Curley

Chapter Summaries

Chapter One: Creating a new landscape

We are in the midst of a great paradigm shift in understanding new models for grief. Scientific data now suggests the process is not what we have been taught.

Chapter Two: Resisting a one-size-fits-all model

A task approach to loss can be detrimental to our emotional and spiritual well-being. This chapter debunks the stages and steps, and the "one size fits all" attitude towards those who grieve.

Chapter Three: Rewriting the script

We need to rewrite the script as we go through grief, taking into account our personalities, background, families, beliefs and much more.

Chapter Four: Questioning assumptions

How we mourn has a profound influence on our psychological and spiritual perceptions. This chapter focuses on funeral homes, and questions the assumptions we have about what is necessary during the time of death and burial.

Chapter Five: Rebuilding our shattered world

Loss is often a beginning. We are resilient in ways we may not have imagined. We can revise, adapt and create again. There is "tragic optimism" that confirms meaning and purpose.

Chapter Six: Embracing the disenfranchised

Cultural justice and genuine empathy are lacking in many segments of our society. This chapter focuses on how we cannot compound loss by ignoring and overlooking grief among the most vulnerable.

Chapter Seven: Crossing life's thresholds via rituals

We cross many thresholds and need to find meaning while we do so. Rituals as vehicles connect us with one another and with those with whom we have an eternal bond.

Chapter Eight: Healing with a compassionate listener

This chapter summarizes the importance of shaping our grief with a loving listener. The importance of "transpersonal" healing through empathic listening is a way of going through grief in a meaningful way. Creative responses bring restoration and new discoveries into our lives.

Chapter Nine: Expressing ourselves through prayer

Grief yearns for context. Religion can provide a context when there are life changing events. We cry out and seek meaning. We look to the faith of the psalmists and their contribution to the Judeo/Christian hopes for rebuilding our lives.

Chapter One: Creating a new landscape

"It certainly seems time to move beyond our current habit of using untested theories to create unnecessarily lengthy-and agonizing models for coping with grief. Tony Walter [1]

We need to reframe the way we grieve and help others through the grieving process. A revolutionary paradigm shift is occurring, based upon research that more accurately portrays this fundamental human experience. It is now time to challenge and embrace more accurate methods. This new approach is necessary, especially for those who are suffering from losses due to a myriad of factors beyond loss of a loved one. These include chronic illness, violence, economic insecurity and other life events that cause deep grief and sorrow.

An intensely psychological approach to life's losses began with Sigmund Freud. Freud did not actually develop a theory about how we process grief, but he established the foundation for future European and American theories about how we resolve our losses.

Since 1917 multiple theories concerning how we process grief have surfaced. Now many of these theories have given way to a dynamically different approach to one of life's most basic emotions.

Freud suffered deep grief at the death of his daughter, Sophie. He made it known that after her death he could not go on as before. He wrote about this in a letter to his friend

Ludwig Binswanger after he learned that his friend had lost his son.

Freud described his deep sense of loss and explained how he would never find a substitute for his daughter Sophie.

Yet those who followed Freud in developing theories about grief for the past seventy-five years have written about "reinvesting" our psychic energy in new relationships as we detach from those we've lost. This is contrary to Freud's personal experience with grief, which is well documented.

This book is about this massive paradigm shift in a perspective that can help us understand our own feelings of loss, while we care for those who are suffering losses as well. When we discuss grief, loss of a loved one through death quickly comes to mind. But we must also realize that life is comprised of many different types of loss, including loss of jobs and economic stability, good health, and love, through divorce or betrayal. All these losses make us grieve and require compassion and empathy.

The primary focus for those in bereavement care is to assist those who have lost a loved one. Yet our new theories are applicable to other types of loss as well.

Different theories have emphasized different aspects of loss. Yet I have always had some deep yearning to more fully comprehend the psychology of loss.

The "let go" and "move on" approach always bothered me because it seemed to diminish the meaning of mourning. In my writing, lectures, workshops and being with the bereaved I felt that there was something simplistic about the phrase, "letting go," one of the most popular dictates for processing loss in our society.

I believed there was more to the story. Often I would qualify that we "let go" in order to reconnect and establish a new spiritual bond and an ongoing relationship with those whom we've lost.

But most of the literature and theories about grief emphasize the "severing" of "affectional" ties. This is in keeping with Freud's approach of letting go of an object and "reinvesting" our energy with a new object.

When we apply this to the death of a loved one, it is more than difficult to reconcile this with eternal life. It also undermines our cherished relationships. It characterizes them as ephemeral. What I believe now is creating an enduring bond.

This book is written in light of the new research and modern methods of data gathering and interviewing that supports an understanding of an ongoing impenetrable bond between those whom we have loved and lost. Now we must emphasize ways to remember in the context of meaning. Now there is finally a dialogue that can take place between science and spirituality. It is now permissible to explore new frameworks that incorporate meaning into our analysis of coping with bereavement

We are facing the great challenge of bridging the gap between research and the way we care for those who are grieving.

How do we actually go through grief?

We will examine the standard practices still employed by many counselors and caregivers, along with their pitfalls.

When we dismantle the old approaches we can then reconstruct the new.

In recent years researchers have debated the effectiveness of the traditional models of bereavement. They have been working in the field of stress and have developed new models helping people cope with loss in their life.

In 1999 Stroebe and Schut published the *Dual Processing Model,* which is revolutionizing our understanding about how we process stress in our lives. The model focuses on our loss orientation and our reconstructive orientation. [3]This model helps us find ways we revise our shattered world and rebuild our new world. For example, it helps widows distinguish between what is constructive and destructive while they are grieving.

I often tell my students we need a well equipped "tool box" to share healing approaches with those whose lives are shattered by loss. When we keep using the same old tools, which have been stuffed under our sink for generations, they get rusty and often don't work.

We can no longer apply outdated and harmful approaches that will not bring hope and understanding for the bereaved.

Over the past century we've amassed many thousands of books, tapes, CDs, DVDs, and lectures to help those who are grieving. New internet technology makes it easy to access resources. But most of them mimic outdated theories. Grief is too important an emotion to be left in the hands of those who just want to recycle old notions, unsupported by the latest scientific data.

The changing landscape

Up until now there have been many theories and numerous publications which purport to show us how we grieve. It is interesting to note that they often suggest that grief is unique for each person. Yet, these theories offer a one-size fits-all approach for this highly personal experience. We are told to follow a predetermined roadmap of steps, phases, and tasks in order to grieve correctly. If we digress from the pre-established framework we are often deemed sick or perhaps pathological. In other words, if we are not practicing the grief program, even though we are unique, we are outside the accepted "norm" and not doing well. This has and continues to be the opinion of many professionals, social workers, and pastoral ministers.

Some maintain if we don't adhere to the tasks of grief we are guilty of "avoidance and denial." They insist we must express our emotions and then "move on" with our lives. If we fail to do so then they assert more intensive psychotherapy or counseling may be necessary. Then we become a "patient" for feeling what is utterly natural.

This distorts the human aspects of grief and labels it an illness. This thinking is prevalent and needs to be corrected.

When we visit friends and relatives we consciously or unconsciously make an assessment about how they are doing, how they are "holding-up." We look for certain textbook signs of grief from stereotypical images of what it means to be bereaved. This is called "looking for symptoms." This is the wrong approach, which is not consistent with what we now know about how people actually respond to loss. It does not consider our ability to be resilient and find purpose and meaning in our grief.

Rigid framework

There are actual schemas for grief theories. They consist of a beginning, middle, and end. These are constructed to make sense of the person's loss. The emphasis is upon a journey through negative emotions for the most part. The individual who is grieving has to fit into this contrived framework.

Even though there are many theories that try to make sense of the person's terrible "negative" experience therapists usually follow one theory they have selected. Challenges to the theory take place when the experience does not coincide with what is structured or schematized. Unfortunately, there are those who want to embrace the theory no matter what and make it the norm for practically everyone. It's akin to letting theory dictate the rules rather than use our actual experiences to illuminate the human condition.

Everyone's journey through grief is different, yet we're all still presented with the rumpled old road map through avenues and roads we need no longer need to use. This is one of the practices that must be challenged.

Beyond the status quo

There are many shortcomings to the standard theories. Many theories do not relate to specific people or to the different spans of life during which we experience grief. For example, the very young and the very old are not given attention that meets the griever's experience.

When the very old die it is not always met with shock. Instead there may be relief if they were suffering at the end of life. How the deceased person welcomed and wanted to die is also not factored. Anyone who visits a nursing home may hear some residents say the they want God to take them or that they "want to go home."

We need to challenge the sweeping assumptions about death, dying and the processing of grieving.

We must ask ourselves how the theory views death. Is the grief response always a devastating experience?

Does the theory really show us how to deal or cope with grief according to what is actually being experienced?

We are all dying the minute we are born, so why can't we begin to view death as part of the natural cycle of someone's life?

Throughout this book we will note the "continuing bond" we have with loved ones even in death. Unfortunately, we are culturally conditioned to follow certain erroneous assumptions. These assumptions include how we have funerals for loved ones and how we are "helped" by counselors.

Despite the difficulties, we must begin to reflect and act in different ways when we confront loss, especially those with the death of a loved one. This book focuses on what is wrong with the old theories and how we need to adapt and accommodate our losses in healthy ways.

Challenge these assumptions

• A relationship dies when the person dies. We should sever ties and move forward. (This undermines our eternal bond with our loved ones.)

• We experience grief solely in an individualistic and intra psychic way. (This ignores the relational aspects of loss.)

• Loss is always a negative experience.

We must have new conversations about how we grieve. It is extremely important these conversations take place for our own good and the welfare of those we love.

Science seems to be catching up with how people really go through grief.

The storied approach

It is far better to have a storied approach to our loss. When we tell our story new meaning is created and shared. About twenty years ago I first taught graduate students about life's separations and losses. Recently I came across one student's paper recalling the death of her mother. Looking back at it now I understand with a fresh perspective her emphasis on the continuing bond with her mother. She wrote:

" I lost my mother in a car accident three and half years ago. My sadness, my anger, my horror, my confusion and bewilderment at her sudden death are my tools for continuing to know her. Paradoxically, sadness, horror and all the other intensely painful feelings intact, I have accepted her passing and in doing so I am on the receiving end of a deepening relationship with her. When I am not steeped in my loss, I am often

full of appreciation for all I learned from her. I notice aspects of her that I didn't notice in her lifetime. I notice ways that I am so like her on occasion I think I feel her living life through me. Accepting my loss of her affords me very intimate reflections in which I "accept" or "take in" or "receive" of her all the more.

These feelings force me to reconnect with her and to celebrate her. Ultimately, and to my great surprise, in being with my sadness I find myself on a never ending journey of discovery, a journey in which I discover, or re-discover the profundity of her influence on and in my life. I find also, the wonder of many subtle ways she continues to live. Grieving for my mother has shown me that letting go of her to any greater degree than death has already imposed on me is unnecessary. Death has done the work of mortally separating us. I am left to work it out."

The joy of the new scientific approach to grief is that it puts into words a much clearer picture of what people really feel and go through. My student's response leads to more healing and hopeful ways to live.

New Research

Amazing results came from a survey of widows and widowers, conducted by George Bonanno, professor of clinical psychology at Columbia University's Teachers College. His survey focused on what percentage of widows and widowers recovered quickly from the loss of a spouse. It also explored how they were doing years later as it evaluated the overall well being of the respondents.

Professor Bonanno utilized a long term study entitled: "Changing Lives of Older Couples", from the University of Michigan. Those who lost a spouse had follow-up interviews at six, eighteen, and forty-eight months after the death of their spouse.

The results are startling, much different from how we

have perceived loss among the widowed. There were very few signs of shock, despair, and other grief emotions as little as six months after the loss of spouses.

A decade ago in 2004 Professor Bonanno published the results of his survey in the *Journal of the American Psychologist*[4]. His study was criticized because it did not conform to traditional expectations. Bonanno has since replicated his survey and his resiliency theory is now accepted by professional clinical researchers. This research has shaken the foundation of existing theories and created new structures for understanding grief.

George Bonanno is cited as one of the driving forces in the new science of bereavement. He has helped replace some misguided grief theories that remain popular among practitioners. (These theories include Kubler-Ross's stages of grief.)

Bonanno maintains that some practices in grief and trauma counseling can be more harmful than helpful and must be changed as part of public policy.

Bonanno has authored a book *The Other Side of Sadness: What the New Science of Bereavement Tells Us About Life After a Loss.*[5]

This book introduces new scientific research into the field of bereavement theory. It maintains that human beings possess a "natural resilience" and handle grief differently than has been presumed for many generations. Bonanno's phrase "coping ugly" suggests that grief manifests itself in many forms outside the established norm, and that some may even be perceived to appear abnormal to those embracing old grief models.

There is ongoing research, which instructs us about the nature and effects of grief. The scientific tools range from functional MRI's to surveys, questionnaires, interviews, and samplings. Present research helps with more accuracy in what it means to grieve and mourn. Yet many grief topics still need to be researched.

We are resilient beings

The new science highlights our ability to experience resiliency while we grieve. It does not mean that we do not grieve, and it certainly does not minimize grief. Rather it means, as Professor Bonanno puts it, we are "hard wired" to go through grief probably better than we thought.

Resiliency is the more common response to grief. It is the rule not the exception. This flies in the face of a "medical model," which insists there are "symptoms" of searching, yearning, anger, and possible guilt. It is not necessary to have grief counseling when we do not express these emotions, as the prevailing theory suggested for many years.

Seeking purpose and meaning is the new description of how the bereaved go through losses. More appropriate responses may be searching for meaning and finding meaning. When the person who is grieving is appreciated as the one who makes sense of his world, we give significance to loss. On a deeper level the bereaved are finding highly personal meaning in their experience. This is in keeping with "sorting things out" while we grieve so we can revise and rebuild our world.

Exploring purpose and meaning offers opportunities for greater change and growth. It shows us ways to transform our lives with a new identity in the face of our loss.

Uniqueness of grief

We have noted the acceptance of the uniqueness of grief for practically everyone. We are all different in our responses to loss. What we have called in the past "symptoms" are really descriptions that vary from person to person. Grief then becomes more a personal collage of our feelings.

In 1993 I published my first book entitled: *Console One Another*[6]. I have since then revised the book. I would like to refer to my earlier publication to illustrate how my own thinking about grief has changed. In Appendix A I cite "Grief Observations." On this topic of emotions I wrote:

> *"Initial emotional responses normally include:*
> *Feelings of sadness, anger, loneliness, tiredness,*
> *Shock, numbness, abandonment, anxiety, yearning,*
> *emancipation, relief, irritability, guilt, and emptiness.*
> *The feelings correctly communicate an overall*
> *disorientation and total disruption in our usual way*
> *of feeling as we do our activities of daily living."*

What I wrote then now needs some changes. It has to be more descriptive for revising and rebuilding and certainly not give the impression that everyone feels the same emotions while they grieve. We need to include the way we process our losses and how we find meaning. This processing is aided by our including the creation of a continual or enduring bond with those who have died.

Constructivist theory

This contributes to equipping ourselves with a "toolbox" for the 21st century. In this toolbox we are giving form to our grief. We are creating a new method to finding meaning.

The constructionist theory helps us know others, our selves, and our world. It especially helps us being with the bereaved and becoming more aware of how they are coping with their losses. This certainly colors our relationships and our difficulties and ultimately shapes our world. This speaks strongly to spirituality, which is an essential element when our world is shattered by loss.

The American Psychological Society, reviewing a six part DVD by Professor Robert Niemeyer, a pioneer in the new science of bereavement, describes this approach in the following way:

" Therapists pay close attention to where the client wants to go... During the session the client is central, and the therapist's job is to ask questions that will lead the client toward his or her own answers, not toward answers the therapist may have. Constructivist refer to this as "leading from one step behind."[7]

This description supports the caregiver as a loving listener for the bereaved. A supportive presence allows the bereaved to take the central place.

Professional referrals are initiated only when there is a prolonged grief reaction. (The actual statistics of those in need of professional help is around ten to fifteen percent.) We are realizing any adjustment counseling needed may be due to a pre-existing condition that might affect the way a person grieves.

We do not want to fall into the trap of thinking we have to refer to professional care almost everyone who is facing the sadness of loss.

Catching our breath

This new approach to grief is a breath of fresh air, which we must deeply take during times of separation and loss. We are given the resilience or what in spiritual terms we would call "grace" to go through our times of loss.

Author Thomas Attig captures the spirit of the how we really find new meaning and hope while we grieve. He writes about how we catch our breath in loving separation:

"Nothing is more essential to catching your breath than continuing to dance in separation. Your loved one's life, soul, and spirit still move you. Reweaving memories and legacies-the enduring rewards of your re-lationship-into the web of your life makes you whole again.[8]"

George A. Bonanno's book: *The Other Side of Sadness, What the New Science of Bereavement Tells Us About Life After Loss*,[9] goes beyond conventional wisdom. It debunks theories that do not represent what most of us go through while we grieve. It illustrates how we are "hardwired" to go through the process by providing examples from his re-search.

Standard grief practices

Employs emotional response

Severing of a relationship

Set framework

Meaning not emphasized

Does not promote dialogue with deceased

Private individual emphasis on grief

Steps, stages, phases and tasks

Detaching and relinquishing

Closure and reinvesting energy.

Conservative/psychoanalytic model

Determines wellbeing by progression

Mourning as painful

Need for counseling.

New paradigm practices

Constructivist/ theory of knowing

 Maintaining an ongoing bond

Challenges for unique needs

Emphasis on seeking meaning

Ongoing and everlasting dialogue

Relational/social emphasis

Revising and restoring world

 Mourning/open & evolving

 Transformative/ rebuilding model

Does not always view prolonged grief as illness

Range of effects for mourning/even laughter as a healthy

response

 Personal resilience

This new paradigm is helpful in giving us updated ways to go through grief. Caregivers can utilize this approach to effectively bring meaning to those who are suffering loss.

The tool box: Keep in mind

The way we choose to grieve should be self-directed and reflect our own belief system. Grief is a natural human emotion and should not be treated as a disease to be eradicated.

Chapter discussion

1. What are some of the way we can implement the new science of bereavement in our own lives?

2. How can we relinquish the process of "letting go?"

3. How do we find purpose and meaning in our loss?

Notes:

Chapter Two: Resisting a one-size-fits-all model

"As we relearn the worlds of our experience, we reweave the fabric of our lives and come to a new wholeness. We reshape and restore integrity to our daily lives." Thomas Attig[10]

Bereavement does not have to be a time of extreme confusion. Unfortunately, our society, even among professional caregivers, often puts too much emphasis on what the bereaved must accomplish.

The following example of Fred, a long distance truck driver, illustrates this reality.

Fred sought help from a "standard approach" grief counselor after his wife Julie died. Driving long hours on the road he often wondered if he was grieving correctly and what stage or phase of grief he was in. He wished he could be settled by accomplishing the "works" of grief. The memory of seeing Julie in the casket haunted him. He was told that he had to "reinvest" his emotions in other things in order to "move on". But he didn't know what that meant or how to proceed. Thinking about the good times he and Julie shared felt right, but he feared he was dwelling on the past. He wished he did not have to let go of the good images along with the bad.

In order to appreciate the true impact of new approaches for grief we have to first deconstruct what has been presented as true for many years. We need to look at the standard way of doing things in our society. Helping ourselves and others means that we become knowledgeable of the many pitfalls in modern counseling.

A medical model for grief is not accurate. Most of us who grieve are experiencing a natural occurrence, which all of us must go through at one time or another in our lives.

I recently had lunch with a couple who had tragically lost their son. They told me how they are finally doing better a year after his death. Initially they had sought out different support groups. After each session they left the group much unhappier than before the session started. They finally stopped going and found themselves beginning to heal. The constant going over the circumstances of their loss was not much help. If anything it made matters worse. This approach for "grief work" or the "work of mourning" is highly ineffective.

Caring support groups

A caring support group has great potential for helping and not harming participants. This is on the condition that the group approaches grief in ways that are healing and helpful. Participants who are expected to follow the standard way of doing "grief work" will only be disappointed.

A caring support group can utilize the new scientific findings about creating a continual bond.

During the past twenty years I have facilitated and co-facilitated many groups. Our format and topics have varied over the years. A parish or temple's group has the objective to help the participants place their loss into the context of their faith. Non-denominational groups can still focus on a person's spirituality.

Some of the topics, which were considered helpful in the past now are seen to be counterproductive. Support groups (which can often be mistaken for group therapy) may have some outdated and actually harmful terms that should be questioned. These include "letting go and "moving on," "going in the direction of the pain," reinvesting our emotions in new relationships," and others which follow certain "tasks" for those who are grieving.

When you meet with facilitators ask what the topics are and how they relate to the way you process your loss. Going over the story of the circumstances of the loss in excessive ways to accept what happened can create difficulty for you. Choose instead facilitators who are present in ways that bring healing and hope and provide opportunities for you to know and appreciate your resilience.

Remembering groups

Author Lorraine Hedtke has published a very innovative approach for support groups. This book invites participants in groups to a new kind of conversation. The conversation is with our loved one who has died. This is in keeping with the new model, which asserts that we have an enduring bond or a continual bond with our loved ones. Instead of having a counselor (and other groups members as well) disconnect the bereaved from those whom they love, the focus in on stories that enhance the connection.[11]

I have always noted how much it affects participants when we ask them to say the name of the loved one they are grieving. We also ask the grieving person to "introduce" the loved one through stories, photos, and other means. This story telling confirms that death does not end our relationship, but sheds a new insight into our new relationship with the person we have lost. The greatest challenge we face is developing an ongoing relationship with our loved ones, while living without them on the material plane. It is not learning how to say good bye. It is learning how to rebuild a different relationship in the context of an enduring bond.

We do need others to be with us in grief and in all of the aspects of our lives. Nobody thrives being alone. The compassion, the socializing, and the caring of others can bring about great comfort. But some people may not need such an approach. Does that mean they are not grieving correctly? Of course not.

Today, we understand that resiliency varies from person to person.

" No culture before has abandoned all recommendations as to how to mourn," notes sociologist Tony Walter. Yet it certainly seems time to move beyond our current habit of using untested theories to create unnecessary lengthy and agonizing models for coping with grief. These have created more anxiety about the experience instead of alleviating it. In *The Truth About Grief,* Ruth Davis Konigsberg has a stunning chapter titled: "The Grief Counseling Industry." She asks whether counseling a person through grief actually works. She similarly questions William Worden's invention of "tasks" necessary for the bereaved.

Standard "tasks"

We need to be familiar with Worden's "tasks" not only for ourselves but for everyone we want to help. The more aware we are of the pitfalls the better we can avoid them. In *Grief Counseling and Grief Therapy,*(4th edition) William Worden lists the "tasks of grief."   The list for this edition includes the following:

1. *Accept the reality of loss.*

2. *Process the pain of grief.*

3. *Adjust to a world without the deceased.*

4. *Find an enduring connection with the deceased in the midst of em barking on a new life.*

It is necessary to critique the popular "task" approach as a model for coping with loss. The overarching question with these tasks is: Does this approach really help us to build meaning in our lives?

Worden first conceived his approach in 1982. Since then he has made revisions to the same basic framework. But I am afraid it is like trying to pour new wine into old wine skins. We must critique his work as his writing is very well known and still popular with mental health professionals.

Task I: Accept the loss

There are difficulties with this first task presented. Certainly there is the need to accept the death. While we relinquish a loved ones physical presence at the same time there are other considerations. What has to be emphasized is that death is not the end of the relationship. I do not find this wording of this task to be comforting. He insists with a case example the necessity to state aloud that the person is dead. There is no mention of the bereaved person's beliefs that he or she may yearn for a reunion in eternal life.

Task II: Process the pain of grief.

The approach here is to go in the direction of the pain. The pain is considered necessary for good grief work. Worden contends that it is necessary to acknowledge and work through pain or it can manifest itself through physical symptoms or some form of aberrant behavior. He quotes Colin Parkes in this regard.

Parkes says: *" If it is necessary for the bereaved person to go through the pain of grief in order to get the grief work done, then anything that continually allows the person to avoid or suppress this pain can be expected to prolong the course of mourning."*[15]

Not long ago I was at a reception with a woman who lost her husband. She really did not expect the loss to happen as quickly as it did even though her husband had been sick for some time. Seated at the table with the new widow and another guest was a pastoral associate whom I had just finished talking to about recent changes in bereavement. The widow spoke about how she felt. The priest, while well meaning, interrupted to tell her it would be very painful to face the future. Needless to say to tell someone that it is only going to get worse is not a good idea. The priest also understood nothing about the woman's personality or how resilient she may be. Later I met with the widow and told her she will receive the strength she needs. I told her not to expect overwhelming pain.

What the well meaning priest said to the widow is the way the theory works or should we say malfunctions. If you tell someone long enough that something will occur it can become a self-fulfilling prophecy. I did not want to leave this grieving woman with that possibility. Certainly there is pain, to be experienced but it doesn't need to be excessive. Amplifying the pain does not help us revise and rebuild our lives. Emphasizing grief work can do much more harm than good.

Task III: Adjust to the world without the deceased

Worden suggests three areas of adjustment. He believes there are external adjustments, internal adjustments and spiritual adjustments.

When things are broken up this way we can easily see that the bereaved are being told "here is what to expect."

Worden actually sets a limit of around three to four months as a time for the realization that one is living alone. Is there any data to indicate that is what everyone feels or realizes? The internal adjustment again presents the issue that self-esteem is affected by the loss of some relationships. Is there any rationale for believing that someone else to this extent validates us? This is seen as an attachment, which harms a grieving person's self-esteem. What is the scientific basis for such an assertion?

The "spiritual adjustment" is described in the following words:

> "Loss through death can challenge one's fundamental life values and philosophical beliefs-beliefs that are influenced by our families, peers, education, and religion as well as life experiences. It is not unusual for the bereaved to feel that they have lost direction in life."[16]

This is a far cry from looking to our resources to provide deep meaning and hope while we grieve. Making sense and sorting things out is done in relation to others. Our religion or our spirituality taps resources for meaning and how we relate to suffering in our lives. The very definition of religion flows from the Latin word "religere," which means to tie together. It is in reference to binding together the supernatural and natural realities. It can similarly tie together our ways for finding meaning.

Worden does stipulate that not all deaths challenge one's belief. He uses as an example the death of an elderly person. After living a well lived life we may not be challenged. So, for the most part he seems to indicate that there is a challenge rather than a consolation for future hope. What is the driving force here?

Task IV: Find an enduring connection with the deceased in the midst of embarking on a new life.

In this fourth edition we see that Worden is influenced by new scientific findings. He has changed the last task from cutting ourselves off or completely severing a bond to the deceased. He quotes Freud :

"Mourning has quite a precise physical task to perform; its function is to detach the survivor's hopes and memories from the dead."[17]

Despite Worden's gesture about connection his framework still focuses on structuring and organizing our feelings around a set task.

He writes:

"It is difficult to find a phrase that adequately defines the non completion of Task IV, but I think the best description would be perhaps "not love."

The fourth task is hindered by holding on to the past attachments rather than going on and forming new ones."[18]

This last statement unveils how the task is really seen. It is really a mitigated version of what was put forth by Freud and subsequently still insisted on for all these years. While Worden does not hold tightly to stages and even warns young counselors to avoid doing that, he still mentions time spans and the roadmap approach to grief. He does mention "dual processing of grief" and believes that his tasks are compatible. But from what I see his approach to grief is still removed from our present understanding of new ways to process grief. Worden is still presenting the argument of saying good bye forever.

The tool box: Keep in mind

The "enduring bond" has been cited a number of times in our understanding of the changing paradigm. There are many influences for this enduring bond. It is different for everyone.

Chapter discussion

1. Do you see any shortcomings in the way the standard theories take people through loss?

2. Do you agree that that tasks must be completed to grieve ?

3. How does disengaging differ from creating an enduring bond?

Chapter Three: Rewriting the script

"Sorrow fully accepted brings its own gifts. For there is alchemy in sorrow. It can be transmuted into wisdom, which if it does not bring joy, can yet bring happiness." Pearl S. Buck

My friend Helen told me she went to a workshop on new approaches to grief. She thought she would obtain information about how to do her grief 'work' according to phases, stages, and tasks. Instead she became aware of an intensely personal way to experience loss. She told me this helped with the death or her mother, and the loss of her job. She said she finally learned to focus on her challenges instead of her symptoms.

Robert Niemeyer in his book: *Lessons of Loss: A Guide to Coping skillfully,* writes about the way to reformulate and expand "tasks" as a set of "challenges."[22] No longer does he use the work "tasks." Instead he offers ways to "relearn" lessons of loss in each new life context, just as the boy who grieves his father's death at age eleven may do so again in adulthood, perhaps when his own son reaches that age.[23]

Learning the lessons of loss

Niemeyer takes us through a series of challenges for the bereaved. These contrast with the standard theory which has been adhered to far too long. [24]

Niemeyer is aware that loss does not happen in a vacuum.

He mentions including children, if there are any, and stresses the importance of a family's beliefs about death and the afterlife.

Niemeyer writes about the initial reaction of numbness or distancing ourselves from pain. He reminds us that bereaved people need private reflection and interaction with others to sort out their feelings. He asks a series of questions among them is: "Does a wave of anxiety suggest the need to seek solace in prayer?"[25] It is comforting to hear this question being asked in the context of the new science.

Revising and rebuilding

It is when Niemeyer theorizes about focusing on the pain that we can see the stark difference from the old approach. He writes: "focusing relentlessly on the pain of loss can be a bit like staring unblinking at the sun. It may actually be damaging if our gaze is sustained too long."[26] He goes on to describe the process of grieving as fluctuating between feeling and doing. This is in keeping with a dual processing of our losses. This model gives us the insight to the importance of how we go through grief in ways that revise our shattered world (focusing on loss) and rebuild and relearn our new world (focus on restoring). We oscillate between the two approaches. It is a far more accurate depiction of the way we grieve. Absent are the old models which had diagrams, invariant steps, phases, and took a linear approach to bereavement. There are not set stages and contrived times in this model.

The researcher George Bonanno also gives us valuable insight to help our understanding of the oscillation with grief reactions. He succinctly places grief into its rightful context:

"Bereavement is essentially a stress reaction, an attempt by our minds and bodies to deal with the perception of threat to our well-being. And like any stress reaction, it is not uniform or static. Relentless grief would be overwhelming. Grief is tolerable, actually, only because it comes and goes in a kind of oscillation. We move back and forth emotionally. We focus on the pain of the loss, its implications, its meanings, and then our minds swing back toward the immediate world, other people, and what is going on in the present. We temporarily lighten up and reconnect with those around us. Then we dive back down and continue the process of mourning."[2]

Life cycles

Bonanno elaborates on how we should not be amazed at this reaction as it is consistent with just about every other back and forth mind body fluctuation. It is how we inhale and exhale, muscles tighten and relax, our body temperatures go up and down, we are asleep and awake. Bonanno makes the pointed observation that "we cannot reflect the reality of loss and engage the world around us at the same time, so we do that in cycles too."[28]

Being aware of oscillation is an important observation for understanding the new paradigm. It refutes the predictable sequential stages, phases and tasks. This is a new way of thinking about grief and stressors. Coping effectively entails oscillating between two separate processes. We fluctuate back and forth. Eventually we regain our balance.

When we process our grief with this dual processing model we must try not to give more attention to one aspect Initially it seems that the revising is emphasized. When we experience the rebuilding and restoring a balance can occur.

Robert Neimeyer's pioneering work: *Lessons of Loss: A Guide to Coping*, has an interesting cover. It is a photo of "Separation" by Edvard Munch, the Norwegian symbolist painter,who painted "The Scream," which sold for $120, million at auction.

"Separation" depicts an almost mystical portrayal of a relationship. There is a man holding his heart which may indicate heartbreak while looking away from a ghostly silhouette of a woman, who may symbolize his haunted memories. The picture embodies the reality of heartbreak.

Another painting by Edvard Munch is noted in the context of life's separations. It is titled: *"The Death Chamber"* which describes a sick room after someone has died. This scene is about his young sister's death years ago. What is interesting is that the focus is not on the deceased but rather on those who survived. In his expressionist approach Munch paints a picture of six people and how they express and absorb the first impact of loss.

Author Thomas Attig uses this painting to illustrate the separation and aloneness each figure feels. He gives a fine description of the scene in his preface to *How We Grieve,*

Relearning the World.

" Although the room is filled with people, in the painting, it seems not at all crowded. Each figure is very much alone in his or her experience of what has just happened. Each is bereaved-deprived of the presence of one with whom he or she has shared life but a few moments before. No one speaks. No one faces, much less approaches, another. None touch or embrace. Each is stunned and still frozen in place and lifeless. Each is withdrawn and vulnerable, reacting in isolation. Each recoils from the death and from the changed reality he or she now confronts. Each is suspended between the world as it was and the world as it is now, transformed utterly by death".[29]

We certainly are wounded in our experience of loss. How well we do in healing our wounds and hurts depends upon our ways of getting outside of ourselves. We need to transcend to accept and continue in our lives. This is no easy challenge for any of us. When we believe we are in solidarity with those who are the living and those who have crossed over the waters of death we can start to relearn our world.

Reconstruct your relationship to that what has been lost.

This challenge reminds me of a story from one of my books on managing loss. It is a story conveying the important relationships have in our lives. We find meaning in our world through our life's connections.

The story is about a father trying to keep his young son occupied. He decided to cut up pieces of a magazine with an image of the world on one side. This global picture would serve as a puzzle and occupy the child. No sooner had the father started on his own project than he heard his son tell him that he had finished the puzzle. The father was amazed. He asked how he did this so quickly. "It was easy," his son told him. On the other side of page was a picture of a man and woman. He told his father: "When I put them together the world came together too".[30]

This story relates to our separations and attachments. If we put together our relationships with others then our world will come together.

This is the challenge when we relearn and revise our world. In terms of our spiritual response this speaks to ways to develop, almost mystically, a new relationship.

A prime example of what it means to loose someone we love is given by C.S. Lewis in his book *A Grief Observed*.[31] It is about the death of his wife Joy Gresham after her struggle with cancer. This book is a powerful lament for our day. It "illuminates the darkness and shows a way forward."[32]

Ronan Dodd gave a provocative presentation about the C.S. Lewis experience at the Dromineer Literary Festival:

"The broken hearted author is alone in his study. We watch, we listen, as this literary giant, a prince of prose, an intellectual leviathan, struggles valiantly to construct order out of wreckage of disconnected thoughts; to summon the energy to shake off grief and come to terms with the death of his wife."[33]

A Grief Observed serves as another pathway assisting us to be more empathic toward such an overwhelming loss and heartbreak. The search for meaning and finding meaning are throughout the book. Insights about our new grief awareness are evident. This is so important for our understanding of the role of sadness while we grieve. It is sadness which "turns our attention so that we can take stock and adjust."[34]

Thomas Attig's words give us insight as to how we have to not sever rather continue our bonds in a renewed way.

"There is the grief work of revising, rethinking and reweaving our loved ones into our lives. We relearn our lives and give our loved ones the everlasting love we have in our lives forever.[35]"

Reinvention

We need to reinvent ourselves in a new world. I'm thinking of lyrics from an old song by the band known as The Seekers.

"You will be my someone forever and a day...If I should ever lose you, I don't know what I'll do."

In the darkness and doubt, which comes from grief we become a changed person with a vision of a new world. Initially we may not know what to do with our lives. There is, however, a strength that will be given to us. This reminds me of the Latin phrase "Debita Vobis." "It will be given to you."

In his last challenge Robert Neimeyer ends the chapter with the "Serenity Prayer" by Reinhold Niebuhr.

"God grant me the serenity to accept the things I cannot change, the courage to change the things I can, And the wisdom to know the difference."[36]

Tool box: Keep in mind

Being with the bereaved means being mindful of challenges they face. It is a time of darkness and also discovery. Our presence assists them in sorting out their lives. `We want to emphasize the continual not severed relationship.

Chapter discussion

1. How do challenges differ from "tasks'?

2. How do you perceive the healing aspects of challenges?

3. How does this new model differ from a task oriented approach?

Notes:

Chapter Four: Question assumptions

"Most adult Americans know nothing truthful about death, dying and funerals..."We know more about buying a DVD player, a plasma TV or a home stereo system than we do about burying our dead."
Joshua Slocum, executive director of Funeral Consumers Alliance

Years ago one of my friends lost her mother and father-in law weeks before giving birth to her son. She accompanied her husband to make funeral arrangements for her husband's father who died of a heart attack, while taking care of his terminally ill wife in a nursing home. My friend and her husband were in their early twenties at the time. They were obviously devastated and confused by death, while preparing for birth.

My friend recalls standing - nine months pregnant - in a casket showroom with her husband being sold different casket packages by the funeral director.

"He told us we needed to pick out something really nice, since it was the last gift we'd ever be able to give," she recalls. In their intense grief they did not realize the funeral director's ploy to make them feel guilty if they opted for something less expensive than the he suggested.

We are most vulnerable when we lose someone we love. When we have to make arrangements for our loved one's funeral we are especially vulnerable. What we do not realize is that from the moment our loved one's body is "removed" by the funeral director the clock is ticking.

Everything after that occurrence is on the clock. It is not

until we speak with the funeral director that the costs of the funeral are actually outlined and payment or payment plans are signed. This time is often characterized by imbalance and uncertainty.

We must look at the landscape of grief we traverse while we grieve. Who is really around to assist us with our needs? Is our well being the major factor in how we are "helped'?

Some practitioners exploit those who grieve. Whether this is intentional or not doesn't matter. The effect is the same. These perpetrators of bad practices include those who "refer" us to "grief counselors," and members of the "funeral industry,"

In 1989 I was writing my dissertation on the then new *Order of Christian Funerals.* I recall mentioning various aspects of the funeral in parish homilies. At that time I focused on the materialistic side of funerals and how the high cost was immoral.

A funeral director, who was previously very friendly, made an appointment to see me. When we met he was indignant and told me he was thinking of calling his lawyer about the things I was saying.

The funeral should not be characterized by excessive ornamentation and unnecessary expenses. Yet if we read the revised version of Jessica Mitford's book titled: *The American Way of Death Revisited*[37] we will be shocked and alarmed by what we continue to do. It is a far cry from finding meaning while we mourn.

In fact it may very well rob us of our meaning.

Mitford describes the undertaker in the following words:

"If the undertaker is the stage manager of the fabulous production that is the American funeral, the stellar role is reserved for the occupant of the open casket. The decor, the stagehands, the supporting cast are all arranged for the most advantageous display of the deceased, without which the rest of the paraphernalia could lose its point-Hamlet without the Prince of Denmark. It is to this end that a fantastic array of costly merchandise and services is pyramided to dazzle the mourners and facilitate the plunder of the next of kin.[38]"

The tone for how we go through grief is set from the very beginning of our loss experience. How well or poorly we do is influenced by how we "sort things out" in a creative and meaningful way. The overarching question for our culture is: "Can we really find meaning and purpose in the way our society structures grief?"

One member of clergy is quoted in the revised edition of Jessica Mitford's book:

"Funeral directors have greater power over the bereaved who put themselves in their hands. It is so sad to see this power turn into manipulation. Attempts to undermine what we are doing, it seems, involve more than the individual funeral director on duty. It seems that Americans have been rendered powerless by the funeral industry. Bright, independent people permit themselves to be moved as if they were mechanical. They are led to their automobiles, from their automobiles to the church, down the aisle to their seat and to the open grave as if they wouldn't otherwise see it."

I have offered many funerals as a priest. Journeying with the bereaved through rituals that make up a funeral is a companionship that I believe brings meaning and hope. But I am uneasy about what I consider a negative contrast to the purpose of rituals.

I am referring to a too commercial approach that most

undertakers adopt. Despite the fact that they are entrepreneurs and often salesman, we have endowed them with the power to minister to the grief-stricken.

The American Way of Death appeared to shake the foundations of the funeral industry at the time. The casket and vault makers, undertakers, embalmers, cemetery and crematorium owners, florists, and even the clergy were upset with Jessica Mitford's revelations. Yet somehow in this 21st Century the funeral director is still the family friend, and we blindly accept the exorbitant price it costs to simply bury someone we love.

Whenever we provide care for the bereaved,we ought to be mindful of social justice. Scripture and social justice are necessary components to minister and care for those in vulnerable positions. Unfortunately, we seldom consider the social justice aspect concerning the expense of funerals.

Parishes should do their own vetting of funeral directors. Local churches should conduct interviews with undertakers and create a dialogue regarding monetary practices. The way our American society conducts funerals is important regarding the expression and management of grief. Caregivers must carefully consider all of this. Caregivers must question the compatibility of the ritual with American funeral practices. Are the two realities at odds? If we look at the intent of the ritual, the answer will be obvious.

The early Christian community played a primary role in the funeral rites. They participated in the care of the deceased's body and were present with the family in the liturgies. This is a far cry from our "sophisticated" way of preparing the body.

Embalming has meant handing over our loved one to the undertaker. The undertaker, who is a technician, assumes great responsibility and control over the way we celebrate the vigil and funerals.

Often the preparation for the wake and funeral is left up to the "professional discretion" of the funeral director, rather than the loving family. When the family goes to the funeral home to make "arrangements," it is as if it is investing in some expensive furniture (caskets/funeral urns) and property (cemetery lots), rather than participating in the burial of a loved one. The cost of a funeral and the lack of involvement in the process is too high a price for families to bear.

Kenneth R. Mitchell and Herbert Anderson[43] have done considerable work in the area of grief. They contend that funerals are designed to create an atmosphere that is at odds with reality.

The authors cite an essay: "The Time My Father Died," by Joseph Matthews, which provides us with an awareness of how a young man felt confronted with burial choices. When Matthews went with his family to make arrangements, he found out that prices varied widely. The family then asked for the lowest-priced casket. The funeral director would not sell it, stating that it was for "paupers." Eventually, the family persuaded the funeral director to let them see the casket.

They saw that it was a simple pine box. Matthew's essay rages about

"...great concealment by means of plush caskets, white satin lining, soft cushions, head pillows, Sunday clothes, cosmetics, perfume flowers, and guaranteed vaults. Empty of symbolic meaning, they serve but to deceive-to simulate life...what a vanity to denude death. All our pretense about it only strengthens its power to destroy lives. Death stripped of meaning and dignity becomes a demon."[44]

The way we prepare the body for the funeral says a great deal about our values concerning death. The denial is evident, along with a materialistic way of doing things, characteristic of our consumer culture. In this context, it is little wonder that in our "business" world the preparation is left to the funeral "industry." Mitchell and Anderson's work contends:

"Any cosmetic work ought to contribute to the proclamation of the gospel rather than be guided merely by the principle of restoring the body to lifelike appearances. For the Christian, the funeral proclaims life through death and not through appearances of life. "[45]

The Catholic archdiocese of Chicago, in its publication: *Now and at The Hour of Our Death*, makes a timely contribution regarding funerals. It cites the words of Robert Hovda, who puts the choosing of the coffin into the liturgical and pastoral outlook:

"The container for the dead body of a believer should be honestly that, and beautiful as simple and well crafted things are beautiful. The liturgical books of the church tell us that "any kind of pomp or display should be avoided." ...The dead body as the sign of the person is what demands honor and reverence, not the coffin.[46]"

The new ritual of Catholic funerals has contributed

to a realization that it should be a spiritual journey, not a fairy tale steeped in denial.

The funeral can and should be be a time of grace. Life's sadness being seen and accepted can give way to the bright promise of immortality.

The way we conduct the funeral with undertakers may well be considered a major "task" being heaped on the bereaved. We are expected to gaze at a loved one in death as if that image will contribute to our memory in a positive way. This fact has never been proven by any data anywhere. There are those who insist that this reaps benefits for the bereaved. Unfortunately, there are those invested in this idea and want us to continue believing their unsubstantiated statements.

In her best selling book entitled: *The Truth About Grief The Myth of Its Five Stages and the New Science of Loss*,[49] Ruth Davis Konigsberg, as an investigative journalist, confronts the "grief counseling industry."

She cites a sociologist by the name of Leroy Bowman who interviewed people regarding the pressure they received during burial arrangements.

Bowman observed the "open casket" supposedly gave families a "memory image." Konigsberg believes it is largely a ploy to increase fees with additional services. She argues that the fabrication of a memory image in the casket is contrived to create a need to keep the body around for three days for embalming and cosmetics and establish the case for an expensive casket and "all the succeeding stages of a 'fine funeral."[50]

I recently received a brochure in the mail from a local funeral home, which is now part of big conglomerate. The wording of the brochure inviting me for a pre-planning guide booklet took my breath away. This advertisement was distributed among many of the cities and towns in my area. The clever copy read:

"Reading the future is impossible, but preparing for it isn't. Too often, death strikes unexpectedly and our families are left to make decisions about our final arrangements when they are not emotionally prepared. That's why preplanning your funeral is so important. It can relieve your family of this unnecessary burden. Think about it—-maybe you owe that to yourself and to those you love."

If I were an older person who worried about becoming a burden to my loved ones, this advertisement would shake me into submission.We need to realize that grief, as an opportunity for commercialization, is rampant in the United States. Many other parts of the world do none of what we do.

By centering ourselves on meaning we place our memories, dreams, and visions into a context that is conducive to our beliefs. This interpretation of reality is far more realistic than the surreal atmosphere of funeral homes. It is better to avoid the funeral home and seek a vigil and other ceremonies in a spiritual place.

The mansion like setting of the funeral home hardly mirrors Jesus' words about the many mansions in his Father's house. Yet the funeral home is probably the most expensive piece of real estate in many communities. Everything is contrived, often to the point of artificiality.

Does all of this really help us to revise our shattered world? Does all of this really help us begin to relearn our world? Does all of this really help us to rebuild our lives?

New questions are surfacing. One major concern is with the "viewing" of the body. This is not something new. In the 1950s, even before Jessica Mitford's investigative journalism, families told the sociologist Bowman about the pressure they felt making the funeral arrangements with the undertaker .[72]

We must continue to question the values of funeral practices. Is there any data that shows how beneficial an open casket is for the bereaved?

Recall how detrimental it can be to focus too long on the loss. The insight about looking at the sun without protection comes to mind. Our gaze fixed on the loss can harm us. We need to go back and forth between loss orientation and restoration orientation. How can it be beneficial to look at our dead loved one, transformed by embalming fluids, lying in the casket? The image here is distorted. We need to question the assumptions, which have been sold to us along with the expensive casket and its elaborate enhancements.

In a support group, an observation by one participant regarding the the wake of his wife summed up what many of us may feel about watching our loved one, embalmed in an open casket.

"She looked really beautiful. But I sat with her for the whole time and it just wasn't her."[73]

There is an implicit agreement with the way we celebrate funerals. There are interventions, which may be employed at the time of the funeral. They are similar to the grief counseling process of repeatedly "revisiting" the death. Tied in with seeing the body is an intervention in talking with the bereaved about the death. Certain questions are asked to promote the mourning process."Can you tell me a little about the death? What happened? What happened that day?"[74]

Despite all of the psychological jargon associated with the funeral and viewing there is not any data concerning how beneficial all of this may be. Again, we are within a framework (Freudian, Neo-Freudian based) which has not up until now been scrutinized according to science.

Reaching out

Rather than engage the bereaved in psychological questioning regarding feelings of loss a better approach can be taken. This does not happen in the funeral home. It may happen during a visit to a bereaved person's home or inside a support group geared toward better ways to cope with losses.

There is nothing in the Christian tradition that dictates that we have to accept this framework for viewing a body for two or three days after it has been embalmed. If anything we could learn from the Jewish celebration of burial before sunset. Prayers are offered and the families come together for a period of time to console one another. Interestingly enough this is similar to early Christian burials long before embalming and the for profit funeral industry..

Jewish burial customs

Let's assess the way funeral preparations and burial are done in the Jewish tradition. It may also have issues with costs, but our focus is on how the burial 'rituals' are different from those we celebrate. Immediately following a death, the deceased are not left unattended. A "shomer" or "watchman" stays with the deceased from the time of death to the burial.

In the traditional Jewish funeral respect is always shown to the deceased. This could account for why the funeral is so soon after the death. It is believed that it is more respectful to have the funeral soon rather than having unnecessary delay.

Viewing the body

It is not a Jewish custom to view the deceased body. Tradition teaches that it is disrespectful to look at a person who can not look back. The practice is to have a closed casket.

There is no viewing except for purposes of identification by the family, if they so desire.

Embalming

The chemical process of preservation are avoided.

Ritual preparation

According to the Star of David Memorial a pious group of men and women may be called in to prepare the body. This is ritual purification washing and dressing the body in a burial garment (shroud) which is usually made of white pure linen. There is a symbolism involved in this clothing. We are all equal in death. The white garment is without pockets which symbolizes we take nothing with us when we leave this world.

Caskets

Tradition calls for a simple wooden casket without metal parts. (Other types are offered now in our contemporary more commercial society.)

Flowers

They are considered frivolous adornments and unnecessary in the traditional Jewish funeral.[75]

There have been studies done on funerals. The focus is on the meaning of the rituals. We have already noted Jessica Mitford and some of her scathing attacks on the funeral industry. It is not just the monetary aspect we have to confront. It is the lack of meaning that also must be addressed if we are to really comfort the bereaved in a spiritual context.

Recently I offered a funeral mass with the cremains (ashes) in the church. I was surprised to see a shoulder high mahogany case transporting the ashes. I asked the funeral director what it was called. He told me it was a "funeral ark." Another person who works in the funeral industry later told me this "ark" has been created to upsell a cremation to compensate for the loss of the cost of a "traditional" casket.

I don't know how this ark came into the the liturgy or what this special touch must have cost. But the price of cremations have skyrocketed.

In the United State it has been the custom for some time to remove the body to a funeral home. This contributes to a sterile and sanitized attitude toward death. This entails considerable problems for meaning and purpose. Other countries in Europe and South America do not follow the custom of embalming.

In Portugal, Italy, Austria, Switzerland and Malta, as well as throughout Central and South America there is no practice of embalming. We have to rethink our funeral practices. We cannot hope to bridge the gap between what we hope is a correct understanding about grief and mourning unless we address this issue.

Tool box: Keep in mind

The practice of embalming our loved ones is not required. Nor are open casket and elaborate funerals. These contrivances have been created by the the funeral " industry."

Chapter discussion

1. What can we learn from interfaith dialogues about burial practices?

2. Is the American way of death in keeping with our spiritual rituals and beliefs?

3. What can we do to change our current way of doing things? How can we help unmask the inappropriate setting and arrangements mandated by the funeral industry and its lobbyists? How can we assist people in ways to emphasize spiritual meaning in our funerals?

Notes:

Chapter Five: Rebuilding our shattered world

"Faith is the strength by which a shattered world shall emerge into the light." Helen Keller

Not too long ago I received a call from an elderly friend, whom I have known for many years. She wanted me to visit her and have some chicken pie, which seems to be the meal of choice in senior housing. I happily agreed and we set a date and time.

Somehow my friend always had a wonderful faith and resilience that I admired. Throughout the years I have kept in contact with her during times of laughter and sadness. The saddest event was when her lovely teenage granddaughter skidded her car into some black ice and was killed.

When I arrived for our visit she confided troubling concern for her son, the father of the teenage girl who died. She told me about the excessive work he does in his neighborhood. During the fall he rakes leaves and in the winter he shovels snow for all of his elderly neighbors. Then in the summer cuts their lawns. She interpreted his actions as distractions, to keep from facing his life and loss. Years ago I would have agreed that there obviously was some kind of denial or avoidance. But, she told me that when she spoke with him he said: "Mother, you have to understand, if I don't do this I can't go on."

My friend's son is an accomplished high school teacher

and continues in his sadness to function very well. He processes his loss by being busy as a distraction and certainly everyday he remembers his deceased daughter.

I told my friend that she should just encourage him to do what he wants. Distractions can be healing. In the standard theories we would have questioned her son's need for extensive therapy. But it is better to realize he is functioning and finding meaning in his life. He lives with sadness and the other side of sadness as well. How we revise or rebuild our world depends so much on our own way of living in the world and discovering new ways to go through life.

Our lives, when we lose a loved one, are very much "like a novel that loses a central supporting character in a middle chapter, the life disrupted by bereavement forces the "author" to envision potentially far reaching changes in plot in order for the story to move forward in an intelligible fashion."[51]

This entails continual revisions in our story and world. Every time our personal world of meaning may be challenged. How can we better equip ourselves for such revisions?

During an interview George Bonanno [52] offers a variety of insights about the science of bereavement. He speaks about the continued connection with loved ones after death.

Discussing his book *The Other Side of Sadness: What the New Science of Bereavement Tells Us About Life After Loss* Bonanno said:

"... I talk quite a bit about people having a continual connection with loved ones after death, and that's been a little bit mystifying. We found that, often it's negative when people have a sense of continued presence. It's often negative, but is also often positive, and like just about everything else with bereavement, there's a wide range of variability here. So some people, if we ask them about such experiences, they'll say that they really don't have anything remotely like that ever in their experience, and other people will immediately lighten up and talk about those experiences. It's very personal, I think."[53]

George Bonanno mentions how people focus on everyday living often not reflecting on the ultimate meaning of life. Bereavement forces us to reconsider our place in creation. Our memories, dreams, reflections are intricate components, which help us make and find meaning.

The psychology of loss teaches us about our relationship with our loved ones in death. It provides meaning about their presence with us. Very often when I offer a reflection at a Vigil service for a family I want to help them with this ongoing bond and presence.

I offer the following words:

"When we loose someone we love they are more present to us than any other time. In death we recall things we perhaps thought long forgotten or insignificant. It may be how our loved one performed a simple *task or a gesture or mannerism, which suddenly becomes vivid. This is what we cherish about how we recall at this time.*"

Some of the recollections over the years evoke laughter and happiness. This is extremely appropriate and cultivates healing for brokenness and pain we feel at this time. I believe this helps the bereaved rebuild their world and revise their relationship.

In my "ministry tool box" it is not avoidance and denial. Rather it is remembering and envisioning a method to continue our story .

Concentration camps and logotherapy

Living in the concentration camps was a shattering experience for prisoners. Yet resilience among some accounted for survival. Some believe that psychiatrist Viktor Frankl's experience in the camp led to his development of logotherapy, the forerunner to a constructionist approach to find meaning and purpose.

The idea of what Frankl called logotherapy originates from the Greek logos (meaning). The psychiatrist prisoner in the concentration camp based his concept on the premise that the "primary motivational force of an individual is to find meaning in life."[56]

Logotherapy focuses on spirituality. It emphasizes our need to embrace the meaning of life. In this therapeutic model clients are given encouragement to confront the logos (meaning) within them. The thrust is on the human responsibility to live in meaningful ways.

Frankl gives a triadic approach with three factors that describe human existence. They are spirituality, freedom, and responsibility. He writes about the defiant power of the human spirit in its ability to tap into the spiritual dimension in order to transcend obstacles in stressful situations. In observations of his time in the camp, Frankl wrote:

"In spite of all the enforced physical and mental primitiveness of the life in a concentration camp, it was possible for spiritual life to deepen. Sensitive people who used rich intellectual life may have suffered much pain...but the damage to their inner selves was less. They were able to retreat from their terrible surroundings to a life of inner riches and spiritual freedom. Only in this way can one explain the apparent paradox that some prisoners of less hardy makeup often seemed to survive camp life better than those of a robust nature.[55]"

Frankl's insight embraces our appreciation of resilience. We can see how Viktor Frankl's theory led to the constructivist approach that allows us to understand the importance of seeking meaning in suffering.

Frankl contends that life under all conditions, even the very worst, still has meaning. We possess the freedom in our lives when we are faced with suffering to still find meaning in what we do. Frankl's account of his interaction with a dying woman in the camp speaks volumes to spirituality and what it means to look forward to eternal life:

"This young woman knew that she would die in the next few days.

But when I talked to her she was cheerful in spite of this knowledge. 'I am grateful that fate has hit me so hard,' she told me. 'In my former life I was spoiled and did not take spiritual accomplishments seriously.' Pointing through the window of the hut, she said, 'This tree here is the only friend I have in my loneliness.' Through that window she could see just one branch of a chestnut tree, and on the branch were two blossoms. 'I often talk to this tree,' she said to me. I was startled and didn't quite know how to take her words. Was she delirious? Did she have occasional hallucinations? Anxiously I asked her if the tree replied. 'Yes.' What did it say to her? She answered, 'It said to me, I am here-I am here-I am life, eternal life..'' [57]

Frankl informs us that "humor was another of the souls weapons in the fight for self-preservation." [58]

A chapter in Frankl's book: *Man's Search For Meaning.* [59] is titled: "The Case for a Tragic Optimism." In this chapter he asks the question: "How does a human being go about finding meaning? He refers to psychologist Charlotte Buhler who observed we can learn from the people whose lives have demonstrated meaning." [60]

There are many examples of those who possess the resiliency and meaning in the face of overwhelming events. These people can inspire us in our own times of suffering.

From cloister to concentration camp

Seventy years ago on August 9, 1942 Edith Stein died in the Auschwitz concentration camp. She is a remarkable example of finding and making meaning in her shattered world. Stein entered the Carmelite convent in Cologne, Germany, taking the name Sr. Teresa Benedicta of the Cross. The case could have been made that she was baptized a Christian and should be released from the camp.

Instead she found meaning in her solidarity with other Jews who were suffering. She refused to be singled out and released. Pope John Paul II proclaimed this remarkable sister and philosopher a saint on October 11, 1998.

Maximilian Kolbe's devotion to others

Another saint from the concentration camps is Maximilian Kolbe, a devoted Franciscan Friar, who became an inmate at Auschwitz in May of 1941. He selflessly ministered to the others in the death camp. He constantly went without in order to share his ration of food.

When ten prisoners were selected for death by starvation as punishment for the escape of three inmates the kind Franciscan persuaded the Nazi officer in charge to allow him to take the place of one doomed man so that that prisoner could maintain some hope of being with his family again. During the two weeks before his death he supported with prayer and song his fellow prisoners. The execution was by lethal injection on August 14′ 1941. This is another example from the death camps of World War II where we experience the making of and reception of meaning amidst suffering.

Tragic optimism

This model certainly applies to our new understanding of

bereavement. The lives previously mentioned illustrate the reality of "tragic optimism." Frankl refers to this as optimism in the face of tragedy.

It illustrates the best in human potential as the kind of hope that weathers the worst of disasters and other turmoils in life. We as a world community have witnessed this tragic optimism after natural disasters, and terrorists attacks, as victims and their families revise and rebuild their lives.

The characteristics of tragic optimism include acceptance, affirmation, courage, faith, and self-transcendence. These are all qualities which are incorporated in the new approaches to grief, logotherapy and a meaning centered counseling. This type of counseling equips clients with strategies and skills which enable them to see themselves in a new light and live out their lives with purpose."[63]

There is also the story about Jerry Long cited by Viktor Frankl. He talked about how Jerry had been paralyzed from the neck down after a driving accident which rendered him a quadriplegic at seventeen years old.

Long wrote to wrote Frankl:

"I view my life as being abundant with meaning and purpose. The attitude that I adopted on that fateful day has become my personal credo for life: I broke my neck, it didn't break me."[64]

Tears and laughter

Developing a sense of humor while living in the concentration camp was for Frankl a life skill. He recounts how he and others made up and told stories to cultivate humor.

George Bonanno stresses the importance of positive emotions. He rightly notes that historically positive emotions received almost no attention in bereavement literature.[65]

I remember writing an editorial response about laughter in church during the remembrance. I was skeptical about how appropriate or healing it could possibly be to a grieving family. At the time some friends told me that they found comfort in laughter. Now, if I could retract the editorial I would. Many years later, especially in light of recent studies, I understand humor's significance.

The research on grief and laughter includes recognizing positive emotion in the facial expressions. It notes that laughter is contagious. It appears that what elicits smiles, helps healing. In his research Bonanno discovered that smiling among widows and widowers, especially early on in their grief, contributed to their overall mental health. This could have something to do with meeting positive people who energize and create happiness. It makes sense that we seek purpose and meaning for the future. A partner who helps is a healing encounter, which often leads to another marriage.

Our culture tends to be insensitive when this happens. It

sets constraints and time limits concerning new romantic relationships. These are often counter productive to how we create meaning and heal while we still grieve. Forging new relationships does not in any way diminish the intimacy we shared with the loved one we lost.

The important question about our sadness and the other side of it is posed by George Bonanno: "How can grief be dominated by sadness and longing, on the one hand, and include frequent smiles and laughter, on the other?"[67]

It is all in how we grieve. When we oscillate between sadness and laughter we are engaging in ways of revising and rebuilding. We are processing our grief not according to the "standard theories." This illustrates again how dynamic and drastic the grief paradigm is for us. A detailed treatment of the dual processing model of coping with bereavement is presented by researchers, which explains how we do oscillate in our ways of coping. When we become familiar with this we can listen more sensitively and be more in tune with how the actual processing occurs. We are given insights as to how we really cry and mourn our losses with two types of stressors: the loss orientation and restoration orientation. Our orientation equips us with ways to make major adjustments in our lives.[68]

Relearning our world

The words of Thomas Attig apply to our stories of loss. He puts into perspective what it means to live and go on in our lives. The challenges we face in loss are evident as we continue being and acting in the world.

"Relearning the world after someone we love died is not a matter of taking in information or mastering ideas or theories. It is rather, a matter of leaning again how to be and act in the world without those we love by our sides".[69]

Tool box: Keep in mind

We are both meaning makers and meaning finders. Meaning reconstruction is a key to appreciating how the bereaved go through grief. This applies to both sides of sadness. Meaning reconstruction allows us to relearn our world.

Chapter discussion

1. How does oscillating between sadness and laughter help us tolerate grief?

2. Can you cite a time when humor helped the grieving process?

3. How does Viktor Frankl's theory help us live a purpose driven life?

Notes:

"No one ever told me that grief felt so like fear."

— C.S. Lewis, *A Grief Observed*

Chapter Six: Embracing the disenfranchised

"It takes a special courage to acknowledge and adequately mourn when the grief is not socially recognized" - Margaret Mead

Joan always felt optimistic and confident in her social and work life. But after her husband died everything changed. Waiting for a seat in a restaurant a host looked at her and asked "Just one?"

Joan told me the loss of her life partner was devastating enough, but now she feels another kind of loss as a young widow, who is sometimes invisible in a world of couples.

Liz had three miscarriages, and has just been told she cannot have children. Yet uninformed strangers and even some business associates continually ask her when she and her husband plan to start a family.

We experience a wide range of losses in our lives, which are not always death related. These include illness, unemployment, economic hardship, divorce, disabilities, and feelings of betrayal from friends and family. Some segments of society often experience what is described as "disenfranchised grief."

The concept of disenfranchised grief was proposed by clinical psychologist Ken Doka in 1989. He asserts that grief can be disenfranchised in three primary ways: the relationship is not recognized, the loss is not recognized, or the griever is not recognized."[91]

We all possess a history of loss. Many of us can pinpoint instances of disenfranchised grief, where we felt alone and ignored or even ridiculed for mourning something. This emotional intensity affects how we interpret our lives and find meaning and purpose again.

Our culture contributes to feelings of disenfranchisement. It does not acknowledge the losses of some people who are often deemed invisible or devalued as human beings because they are not part of the mainstream. These include minorities of all kinds. Their feelings are often discounted; their spirits not part of the analysis. This plays itself more than we realize in our society. Unfortunately, disenfranchising those who do not conform has become an acceptable way of behavior.

Failure to empathize

There are multiple instances of how disenfranchised grief affects people. It devalues a person's spirit and often diminishes or destroys meaning.

Ironically, professionals, such as medical doctors, mental health counselors and even social workers sometimes contribute to feelings of disenfranchised grief. Like certain members of society, they pride themselves in remaining detached from others suffering, preferring to keep a cool, even critical eye when genuine empathy is needed.

There are differences as to how we engage one another.

Sympathy is the offering of condolences: "I am sorry for your loss." Empathy is the sensitive engaging response: "It must be difficult for you." When we empathize we place ourselves in the other person's position, and that person feels comfort that another human being is aware of the loss and genuinely cares about consolation.

Bereavement and the bereaved

Both bereavement and bereaved are words that derive from a verb not very often used today in colloquial English. The word is "reave" means "to despoil, rob, or forcibly deprive." This, according to Doka, indicates that the "stolen person or object was a valued one and suggests that the deprivation has harmed or done violence to the bereaved person."[92]

When grief is overlooked, discounted, or ignored, this creates an added burden that prohibits those grieving from revising and rebuilding their lives.

A separate mind

Mental illness is still considered a taboo in our culture. Many societies have marginalized those who suffer from mental illness. Communities do not receive appropriations needed for professional programs and services, and we continue to stigmatize those have mental illness, with Hollywood stereotyping. This compounds the loss for the person who has health problems.

Author Benjamin Boone addresses the issue of "living loss" in his book, *Minority of Mind.* [93] Boone, who was diagnosed with schizophrenia the day after he graduated from Emerson College with writing and publishing degree, shares his experience with insensitive treaters and society stereotypes. Yet he sends a message of hope to others in his examples of rebuilding within the constraints of illness.

Boone writes:

"But I can focus on what happens inside, away from my clouded mind. I can be part of society and contribute by living a dedicated life, even when society's purpose and progress are off course. I have heard many people's stories that made me realize the universality of the human experience. We all face adversity in different ways. Pain should not be ignored in a public display of privilege. Our hardship should be shared. This is the only way to make sense of the human struggle and give meaning to mental health."[94]

Misuse of power

Ken Doka cites multiple incidents of abusive ways people are not recognized as grieving" He notes two incidents regarding "disenfranchised grief in caretakers."[95] They describe how physicians fail to respond to sorrow. Certainly, this does not apply to all. Yet, many of us have experiences that illustrate a lack of empathy.

The husband of my dear friend Marian was recently diagnosed with terminal cancer. For months doctors assured her husband that nothing was seriously wrong with him, despite some debilitating symptoms. Finally, during what was to be a relatively simple surgery it was discovered he had a rare type of cancer that had metastasized. A week later Marian kept an appointment for her annual physical with her doctor. She mentioned her husband's shocking stage four cancer diagnosis, then broke down and began to sob. Rather than provide any comfort, Marian's doctor coolly asked her if she wanted a psychiatric referral to get a prescription for a mood elevator. Marian didn't need drugs, she just needed another human being to reach out and acknowledge her pain.

Misuse of power and position triggers the disenfranchisement and hinders a person's ability to cope with loss. Often this extends beyond a simple failure to empathize and even includes anger and impatience directed towards those who grieve. In the extreme it includes blaming or even scapegoating the person who is grieving.

Children and loss

There are many more books about children and loss. Great strides have been made to develop ways to help them grieve their losses. Previous studies about how children grieve were often retrospective. This means that studies were done with adults looking back to their childhood in the context of a therapy session. More recently children are actually observed via expressive therapies that include art and music. Yet, children still remain in many ways excluded from our understanding of grief.

In our families we all have stories of how children react to loss. I recall my very young twin nieces' behavior when their mother was in the hospital for an operation. They decided not to eat, until they could see their mother again. My five year old nephew, reacting to the sudden death of his grandfather suddenly asked me one day: "Did that man who used to live here like this?" Children do grieve and when we acknowledge it we can relate to them and their loss in ways that also help them relearn and rebuild their young world.

In the past we often viewed the loss children feel as a subtext of our adult losses. But new research suggests that children also feel losses that adults in their lives may not even realize or understand. These include peer exclusion, being perceived as "different' from classmates or neighbors, and other feelings of inferiority. Only recently have we as adults begun to address the serious issue of bullying, which can result in child and teenager suicide. The effects include humiliation, fear, social isolation, and loss of self-esteem, illness, and depression.

After Hurricane Sandy hit the New Jersey coast I traveled to New Jersey for a day of prayer and conversing to seek meaning with those who were victims of the disaster.

In the course of our discussions we spoke of trauma and children; how they perceive according to their developmental stages. Shortly after September 11, 2001 young children thought the scenes replaying the Twin Towers destruction on television was actually happening again in real time.

In New Jersey some children expressed panic after the hurricane when they saw trees sway in the wind. During that time together in New Jersey we had no knowledge, as we discussed the program *"Rainbows for God's Children,"* how much it was needed. Soon after tragedy struck at Sandy Hook Elementary School in Connecticut.

Children observe events but cannot always be interpreters of events. Significant adults and how they behave makes all the difference. The child's world consists in age appropriate ways with "magical thinking." They cannot always distinguish between what is real and imaginary. Similar to adults they may need to tell their story over and over again. Perhaps, lacking an emotional vocabulary, it is necessary for children to engage in other ways to communicate their grief. Art therapy is a pathway for the child to express and communicate personal experience. Children need to revise and rebuild their lives perhaps in different ways but essentially this has to happen for them in bereavement. When we are more aware of a child's world we can help him or her cope with losses.

Families and developmental disability

There is only a scarce amount of research on the subject of the death of a child with developmental disability.[96] The study of a support group for mothers who parented and lost children with severe disabilities speaks to the need for these participants not to be ignored or devalued. This study has a real value for understanding how these mothers were revising and rebuilding their lives. It further illustrates the importance of homogeneous groups. Other groups would have members say such things as: "It was better this way," referring to the death of a child who they perceive has been a burden.

Members of the group were asked to write their story. Two assumptions played an important role for the facilitation of the group. They were that there were two major losses: losing the dreamed of child and the loss of the actual child. What emerged for the participants was a sense of identity, priorities, deeper relationships, greater faith, and an extremely different worldview.

Educator Thomas Walsh listed important things to keep in mind when relating to families of children with disabilities. This is a positive approach to insure that there is not the disenfranchisement.[97]

Acknowledge feelings.

Acknowledge the value and purpose the loved ones have placed on this special person.

Acknowledge the special bond among parents, siblings, and the disabled person.

Acknowledge that the parenting of a disabled person is a special gift.

Encourage continual involvement in support groups.

Help them ritualize.

Place loss into religious context

Listen with eyes and ears.

Teenagers and loss

There are many areas where teenagers' grief is not recognized. Important aspects of their development are not always appreciated. They are even trivialized by other generations. Their falling in love is often dismissed as merely "puppy love." The intensity of their feeling are all too often considered "overly dramatic."

Adolescents especially suffer from disenfranchised grief. One of the more noticeable is "celebrity loss." The impact upon the adolescent following the death of a pubic figure is in many instances neglected.

Two prominent celebrity losses - Michael Jackson and Whitney Houston - illustrate the impact celebrities have on young people's lives. One teen described Whitney Houston stating: "She was the sound track of my life." The adolescent years are certainly tumultuous. One psychologist concluded adolescence is "like moving a house with all the furniture in it across the street. You have to expect that everything will be moved around inside." This critical period from childhood to adulthood must be acknowledged, not ignored.

Unfortunately, many caregivers are not equipped to understand this important period in human development. Too frequently the underlying causes of "acting out" are not explored. Expensive for profit residential treatment centers for troubled teens have emerged in the past three decades as lucrative business. Only recently have we begun to re-evaluate these centers, too often run by staff that does not have the education or experience to help troubled teens become well-adjusted adults.

I recently read about one center in Maine that preyed upon youth, charging over $50,000 per student per year. The center, which opened in the 1970s, made millions for its founders until former residents, used social media to shed light on the center's abusive practices. These included forcing residents to fight one another in a boxing ring for punishment, causing the person being punished to fight stronger and more powerful opponents until he or she was defeated, wearing degrading signs, diapers for exhibiting immature behavior, use of isolation cells, withholding of food, and digging and refilling ditches. When the center finally was forced to close in 2011,one former residents blogged: " I have been mourning the childhood I lost. Now I hope I can finally create a new life."

Others were not so lucky. Nobody believed them and they took their own lives.[98]This certainly is a prime example of disenfranchised grief caused by the misuse of power by the abusive treatment center.

Divorce

When a divorce occurs everything changes for the partners involved. Their social network is often shattered. Mutual friends are no longer seen. This is another example of disenfranchised grief.

The new science of bereavement speaks to the way we relate to people who are divorced. All that has been noted about how to be challenged in grief applies to this experience. Applying the standard theories to loss can have some very damaging effects on people's well being. The divorced best respond to the stress of loss by employing a dual process of revising their shattered world and rebuilding a new and different world.

One of my students wrote some time ago what I believe is a fine response to reconstructing life after a divorce. She wrote about her family after a marriage of approximately twenty years failed.

"As I began to be more aware of my changed surroundings, I started practicing rituals with my children to help them understand that our life was different. When they would return from a weekend with their father, we would celebrate our reunion with a formal dinner in the dining room. The children would take turns letting me know what they would like for dinner. I would prepare their favorite foods and we would spend hours talking over dinner. This became important for them as well. It gave me focus for part of my weekend and it was a wonderful time that we knew we would spend together. After doing this for about a year, it no longer was as important for us to do this regularly... but it helped us refocus and rebuild."

Creative ways to respond to loss is always a challenge, but a worthwhile one that can help us rebuild.

Unemployment and economic loss

Our culture and livelihoods are based upon work. Yet after the collapse of Wall Street in 2008, hard working citizens suffered unemployment or lost their businesses. Basic living expenses, such as being able to make monthly mortgage or rent installments, pay for heat, electricity, telephone and gas have become a daily struggle. Entertainment, dining out or taking a vacation are for many no longer possible. Some people have been forced to sell their possessions and when they had nothing left to sell, rely on relatives, who were often struggling themselves.

Worrying abut survival takes its toll, and leads to depression and poor health. Yet our society still favors the successful.

Despite the continuing widespread economic downturn people who are unemployed or poor are still often regarded as inferior people who do not take responsibility for their lives. This victimizing the victim exacerbates the loss, and makes it more difficult to recover and rebuild.

Reducing the Impact of disenfranchisement

There are many instances of disenfranchisement or ignored grief in our society. We must be aware that this exists and that it directly impacts mourning. How we acknowledge or fail to acknowledge what people are enduring in their lives affects the best practices for the new science of bereavement.

We have touched upon just some losses we are concerned with in this chapter. We must be aware of obstacles faced and how they prevent us from moving forward.

Tool box: Keep in mind

We must strive for empathy always. This brings about meaning and purpose in our encounters. Seeking out and embracing those who are often "invisible" in our society gives a voice to their suffering.

Chapter discussion

1. List some instances of disenfranchised grief from your life's journey.2. How does disenfranchisement affect a person's processing of grief?

3. How are different groups affected by unacknowledged grief?

4. How can we better advocate for the disenfranchised?

Notes:

Chapter Seven: Crossing life's thresholds via rituals

"I know of no people for whom the fact of death is not critical, and have no ritual by which to deal with it." Margaret Mead[99]

When my siblings and I were young our father would often come home from work after dark. Before he came into greet us sometimes he would tape lollipops to a bush in our yard. The next morning he looked out of our dining room window and feigned surprise, announcing that the tree had once again sprouted candy. We'd shriek with glee and go out and pick lollipops.

When my father died we all gathered at what had been our family home, and one of us suggested we plant lollipops in our father's memory, and to share the experience with the next generation, his grandchildren. Seeing the excited faces of my nieces and nephews as they discovered the lollipop tree helped us all immortalize my father's sometimes zany spirit and made him present in a deeply personal way. This lightened our grief and helped us reframe our relationship with him for ourselves and others.

When we perform certain ritualistic actions we acknowledge our pain in often productive ways that help us heal.

Rites of passage

A special category for rituals known as the "rites of passage" refers to how individuals transition from one phase to another during the course of their lives. Our understanding about crossing over significant thresholds in our lives is often expressed in rituals with different ceremonies for young and old, male and female, and the living and the dead. [100]

Arnold Van Gennep, a French anthropologist, first used the term 'rites of passage" in 1909. He studied rituals in the life cycle. Events such as childbirth, adolescence, death and many other major occurrences were signified by rituals or set patterns of actions. Through ritual expression we are able to finalize many important changes. At the same time we redefine our relationships as new roles occur. Van Gennep carefully analyzed common life changes.

He actually grouped rituals into three categories he called pre-liminal, liminal, and post-liminal, based on the the Latin word "limen" meaning threshold .[101]

Transitions

Whenever I teach about rituals I make it a point to walk over to the classroom door. When I cross over the threshold I talk about the transition. My action illustrates the pre-liminal, while the actual crossing over is liminal. Post liminal is the new experience we encounter on the other side of the threshold.

The tradition of a husband carrying the bride over the threshold into the home they will share depicts the change the couple is experiencing as they cross into a new personal and social status. This crossing over a threshold can also be applied to the grieving process. We traverse through changes, embark on a new life, yet with oscillations between loss and restoration. We do not always cross over thresholds quickly, but realizing it is a threshold, a certain passage, often helps us to get to the other side more easily.

The value of rituals

Joseph Campbell in his book: *Myths to Live By*, gives his interpretation of the importance of ritual:

"The function of ritual is to give form to human life, not in the way of a mere surface arrangement, but in depth. In ancient times every social occasion was ritually structured and the sense of depth was rendered through the maintenance of a religious tone reserved for the exceptional, very special, sacred occasions. And yet even in the patterns of our secular life, ritual survives. It can be recognized, for example, not only in decorum of courts and regulations of military life, but also in the manners of people sitting down to table together."[102]

Ritual making may entail not only words and gestures but also signs and symbols. Celebrating rituals in action and symbols communicates our ability to go beyond ourselves in ways that explore life's many layers and textures.

Artists, writers, sculptors, and poets have given us many ways to ritualize. Accepting and managing grief is aided by rituals. Rituals are meant to release rather than control our emotions. Very often there is the mistaken opinion that self-control is reinforced by rituals. Nothing is further from the truth.

The ritual is a way to help the bereaved cope with the bereavement experience, as long as it is not viewed as a task.

Grief across cultures

The American-European models for grief drastically differ from other cultures. The models for grief in our societies rely too strongly on the psychological impact of loss and not enough on ritual expression. Other cultures focus on rituals that illustrate an ongoing bond.

An account of the African Shona tribe describes how several months after a death there is the ritual of "hitting the grave." This wakes the spirit of the departed person for the major burial ceremony, which occurs within a year after the death settles the spirit. During the ceremony the spirit of the dead person is invited back home, to re-enter the community.

This may symbolized by a physical journey, such as bringing a goat from the bush back to the homestead.

In the tiny Caribbean island of Carriacou, one of Grenada's sister islands, residents practice the "wetting of the ground," to remember the dead during good times and bad. Whenever a new bottle of alcohol is opened the first few drops are poured on to the ground with some water as an offering to dead relatives and friends. Before having drinks to celebrate birthdays and wedding anniversaries, the ritual of ground wetting invites dead relatives to share with the living.

During times of stress and and uncertainty, a person may also perform this ritual to call up graces and guidance from departed relatives and friends.

Another ritual for Mexicans is known as the "Day of the Dead," (Dia de los muertos") This Mexican holiday is often celebrated throughout the country and around the world with other cultures.[105]   This is an historic tradition, which includes building private altars, honoring the dead by having sugar skulls, marigolds, and a loved one's favorite food or beverage. People also gather at cemeteries to pray for the loved ones soul. (This holiday coincides with the Catholic feasts of All Saints and All Souls in November.)

In Brazil the "Dia de Finados" is a public holiday that many Brazilians observe by visiting churches and cemeteries.

Japanese continual bonds

In Japan the immediate family keeps a night vigil, on the day of death, before the funeral the following day. Most bodies are cremated in Japan. After the cremation, the family and close friends use special chopsticks to collect bone fragments for a cinerary urn, to be placed in a family grave after the funeral. In the Japanese tradition of remembering and honoring the dead, memorial services are sometimes held every seven years on the anniversary of the death.

These are just some of the rituals many cultures celebrate to create an enduring relationship between the living and the dead in the context of eternity.

Robert Neimeyer cites the challenges in the context of ritualizing our losses and how doing so can assist the bereaved. He follows three basic dimensions.

1. **Transformation of the mourner's sense of self.**

This acknowledges changes and notes that one's relationship may be preserved in a symbolic manner. This is in keeping with the Catholic funeral ritual, which states in liturgical prayers "life is not taken away, it is changed." The continuation of life forever after affects the mourner's grief experience.

2. **Transition to a new social status.**

The funeral ritual separates the living and the dead. In the liminal aspect of the ritual we are developing a new relationship with our loved one who is present in the spirit.

3. **Connection to that which is lost**.

This dimension contributes to the enduring bond. It is an alternative to the severing of affectional ties. This belief in an ongoing relationship is evident in subsequent rituals for the mourners.

The coming together for the "month's mind" mass and

the celebrations of certain feasts such as All Souls Day and All Saints give meaning to the ongoing relationship in faith with our loved one's spirit.[108]

Challenges and rituals

Ritualizing our losses expresses our own innermost intimate being. Our discoveries give us new ways to relive and relearn our often shattered reality.

One of my students shared her story about no longer wanting her wedding ring after her divorce. She took a trip to a foreign country and found a place to bury the ring, knowing she would never go back to it. This was her way of adapting to the loss in her life and reorienting herself to a new way of living. She wrote the following account.

The wedding rings

"The most difficult ritual that I experienced regarding my separation was the time I disposed of my wedding rings. I had three rings that made up my wedding ring. A year and a half after the separation, I went on a trip to Morocco. Before I left, I decided I wanted to take them there and dispose of them in such a way that I would never be able to retrieve them. These rings had been put on my finger the day I was married and never taken off until the week he moved out. These rings symbolized my marriage more than any other object I owned. To get rid of these was very difficult. Once I removed them, I never put them back on my finger, but I did look at them often ... I felt getting rid of them would be healing.

While I was in Fez our group was walking through old ruins. I noticed that a brick was loose on the floor of one of the rooms. I stayed in that room until everyone had left. I removed the brick, dug a small hole and placed one ring in it then replaced the brick...A few days later we were in ruins in Voulebelesse. There was a place which was once a room and was now overgrown with weeds and flowers. I decided to leave my second ring in this room. I held my ring in my hand and tossed it into the garden and left. On the last day of my trip I disposed of the last ring in Casablanca. I noticed in a room a potted plant. I went into the room removed some soil, placed the ring in the hole and covered it up.

The entire flight home I had regrets. I knew they were gone forever and I could never get them back. I felt I had made a mistake and that I shouldn't have given them up. But as the days went by and my life's routine took over, I looked back on my decision and knew it was right. Since the rings carried so much significance for me, the burying of the rings was my way of giving another part of my marriage up."

We need to relinquish certain things while we grieve. This moving story speaks to revising our lives, which might entail deconstructing before we can rebuild. It may be painful but ultimately rewarding.

Putting keepsakes in a "memory box" apart from our daily possessions is another way of preserving, but also moving forward. A daily ritual of journal writing is especially helpful as we focus on revising and rebuilding.

Self-Discovery

Writing down our thoughts by journaling brings purpose and meaning. It is an expression and vehicle for our sorrow. The journaling experience helps us to discover ourselves while we are changing and realize how we remember our loved ones. Journal writing has a ritualistic tone for lives seeking harmony.

Tool box: Keep in mind

Rituals are outward expressions of our crossing life's thresholds. In the context of grief they help us recognize transitions and can help us reinvent ourselves and rebuild our lives.

Chapter discussion

1. What rituals help shape and give meaning to our lives?

2. How can we create new rituals that will help us create an enduring bond with those we have lost?

3. What can we learn from rituals in different cultures?

Notes:

Chapter Eight: Healing with a compassionate listener

"He knew what it was like to miss someone. And so he listened. And in his listening,his heart opened wide and then wider still.

-Kate DiCamillo, The Miraculous Journey of Edward Tulane

During times of loss we need to explore many different ways to foster healing. How well we accept and go through critical times depends to a large degree on how we shape our grief.

Selecting someone who can be a "compassionate listener" can make a difference. This person can be a family member or friend who understands the value of listening, without passing judgement on our acts of expression.

We need someone who will be present for us and assist us in revising our shattered world and rebuilding and restoring our lives. The compassionate listener hears our story.

It is obviously important that this listener understands and embraces new models for grief, and does not cling to the old concept that we must go through certain stages and steps. We should select a person who is willing to share our journey and travel with us.

Transpersonal healing becomes evident when we draw strength and the ability to be resilient from someone else. This person is with us to help us reweave the experiences of our losses into the wider tapestry of our lives.

This goes beyond a medical or therapeutic model. This is about trusting another without a map or a framework.

It is our perception of loss with storytelling and images which can give form to what is often the formlessness of grief.

Our selection of a loving listener is someone who cares about our well being and is willing to be present to us while we sort out and struggle with our thoughts and emotions.

It is with good relationships that we are able to recount our stories in creative ways.

It is grace itself when we find someone who is willing to journey with us as we initiate new ways of relating to our loved one who has died or divorced or abandoned us.

This compassionate person is willing to walk through the dark valley in a compassionate and caring way. Friends do this more times than is ever accounted for or reported in our society. Good people do good things for others.

We need to have compatibility in our beliefs with our compassionate listener. Our listener may act as a spiritual as well as emotional guide. Expressing our enduring bond is essential to the story. When we share beliefs with the loving listener we communicate with the listener but also with our loved ones in a new and meaningful manner.

Empathy not sympathy

Sympathy is the expressing of concern and condolences to the bereaved. It is a passing and objective action. We are all familiar with how when we attend a funeral service we may offer our condolences. It is usually one of those more unpleasant and awkward moments in life.

"I am sorry for your loss." Or "Please accept our condolences." are polite phrases in our society. Certainly sympathy is an act of kindness and deserves appreciation. But those who are grieving need more than proper etiquette.

The empathic response is far more involved. Empathy means our imagining ourselves in another's position. It is far more engaging. Some would venture to say that empathy actually entails placing ourselves in the other's position and feeling the pain.

We are present and inviting in our whole empathic approach: "it must be very difficult for you." Unlike sympathy this kind of engaging invites a response. Invariably the bereaved are invited to express feelings. Empathy connects our emotions with the grief stricken.

The compassionate listener has to be one who is sensitive to the differences between empathy and sympathy. An empathic person can bond with the bereaved. The empathic and often spiritual guide can be someone who cares.

It could be a mentor or peer, a teacher or student, close

friend or a new acquaintance. It is not necessary that the person be a professional. This is because grief is not an illness. It is part of the life cycle.

Chaotic yet creative

Experiencing a significant loss, as noted previously, creates a chaotic time. We may feel disoriented and confused. This is especially evident with sudden loss such as an unexpected death, disaster or accident, which shock us beyond belief. To accept the loss means that we need some way of being able to live with it. We need to "make real" what has happened to effectively grieve.

We may well feel alone and unloved. We might not trust our emotions Our hearts are crying out and it may seem no one hears our lament. We are going through the "dark night of the senses and the soul."

At the same time there is the other side to our experience. This may be a period when we can discover new depths to our personalities, the resilience that lays beneath the surface. Oscillating between sadness and even laughter can occur as we revise our life's script.

A dialogue with those we trust can facilitate all of this.

Over the years I am still amazed at the storied approach my students take concerning loss. They are creative and reinforce the legitimacy of our present day findings about grief. My concept of the compassionate or loving listeners has broadened because of them. Now it even incudes some-one who may not b be able to offer feedback, but the spir-itual presence that allows you to speak to them from the deepest recesses of your soul.

One student wrote to her dead father in the following let-ter:

"A couple of times you have come to me in dreams and when I'm awake, I tell myself it's because you are trying to reassure me. Hey, Dad here's a funny story. One day last week I was eating my lunch on top of the spot where your ashes are, and the cemetery security guard drove up and told me to leave because it was against the rules and disrespectful to picnic on people's plots. I was furious and said: 'Oh, can I introduce you to my father? Sorry, he can't shake your had hand right now. He's busy eating his lunch too!' I hope you heard me because I'm sure you would have laughed."

This is an important story. It reveals and ongoing dialogue and enduring bond between those we have loved and lost. It also show also once again the "policing" of the bereaved. This experience became a creative and healing moment for my student.

From darkness to light

Can we go through the grieving process on our own? Of course. But supportive relationships provide a new dimen-sion. Interaction with others usually offers insight about our-selves and how we are approaching the world. It gives us a grounding reality.

Without relationships we do not do well in life and this is

more evident during bereavement.

Searching for meaning

Familiarity with Victor Frankl's logotherapy helps our interactions. Centering our discussions around meaning and meaning making is a model that is conducive for good grief.

Story telling is a way of sorting things out, and finding meaning or purpose. Sometimes we physically act out our searching. We find ourselves going back to familiar places for both ourselves and the departed person. Yearning to be with someone who is separated from us is one of the most intense of all of our emotions. Perhaps traveling with a loving listener, while you recall some familiar anecdotes will help bridge the gap between then and now and help you cross the threshold to healing.

Facing impatience

Usually people are supportive but in limited ways. During funerals and for a brief time afterwards they are willing to talk about loss. This holds true with other losses such as divorce, job loss, and health problems. But after we begin to repeat and retell the story several times, support seems to vanish. Our society does not do well with conversations about life's loses. Loss related topics and conversations are avoided as we noted with "disenfranchised grief"

Selective listening also does not help us during times of loss. When loss occurs some will merely give lip service or perfunctory remarks. It is sad when our tragic experience falls for many on deaf ears.

We should not become despondent when this happens. It is a human reaction. We should also realize an underlying belief in the stringent timelines our culture has designated for " grief work" may be at play. We should continue, as long as we are trying to sort out our feelings, and revise and rebuild our world. We must never let anyone tell us: " You should be over your grief by now."

In my book: *The Ministry of Consolers*[113] I devoted a chapter to some skills necessary for the compassionate listener. The following are some points to keep in mind if your are called upon to assume this role. You may also share them with those who are journeying with you through grief.

Stay focused: We need to be attentive and not suffer distractions such as watching television or listening to the radio or glancing at a magazine.

Allow the person to speak: The whole idea of listening is defeated when we interrupt a person. Gestures such as placing our hands over our mouth or our chin in our hands can remind us to be quiet.

Don't be judgmental: Being defensive and looking for what is right or wrong does not enhance listening.

Avoid non-verbal signals: Shrugging your shoulders, using a certain tone of voice, loss of eye contact, and rolling your eyes are statements in themselves that communicate a lack of empathetic involvement.

Don't give advice: Eventually you may be asked to give advice. But do not offer it initially unless asked to do so.

Journaling

Another way to be with a loving listener is to have a friend assist you with journaling. This can serve as a healing tool you can share in additon to or in place of conversation. It can offer a positive pathway through grief.

Journal writing is like dieting. There may be compelling reasons to do it. Like dieting, we journal when we are ready, but also like dieting we are urged to begin when there is a need. We shouldn't wait for the problem to overwhelm us and become the driving force in our lives. [115]

Actually beginning is the most important aspect of journaling. My aunt once told I me: "A job started is half finished." Compiling a journal, which we might share with our loving listener may not be too difficult, once we fill that first page.

Of course, if this does not seem right, don't feel pressured. Remember, journaling is a resouce available for you, not a task you must complete.

Here are some tips.

Select your format: This may range from a three ring binder to a computer journal organized according to your preference. A notebook with a colorful image, you can keep by your bed may also be helpful. Choose the medium that feels best for you.

Choose words, images, art or poetry: Certain music, art, and poetry captures special remembrances about a loved one. Photos can be a catalyst to recalling memories of shared times that are now put into a new context.

Journal at a time that is best for you: Select a time of day when you can give fifteen or twenty minutes without inter-ruption. Don't worry about the length of the entry.

Let your expression flow: Openness to our stream of consciousness fosters healing revelations. There occurs a spiritual unveiling which leads us to healing images in the mind. Imagination and healing go hand in hand. We want to mindful of how we process our losses. We may have the os-cillating of images of joy and sorrow.

Share hopes and dreams: We may be feeling the death of dream in relation to a loved one. This may entail part-nership in life's ventures, and other dreams fulfilled or van-quished.

Remember while we grieve we are trying to make sense of everything. Writing and drawing helps us sort things out.

We may want to recall memories, dreams, and reflections.

Grief is a time for self-discovery. We might be amazed at our own resilience. The changes and crossing over thresholds in our lives creates a new identity and helps us relearn our world in more surprisingly rich ways.

We should remember while we are grieving we are facing challenges rather than set tasks.

Tool Box: Keep in mind

Sharing our stories with a compassionate listener can enrich our lives and facilitate healing. These approaches are meaning centered to assist us and others in becoming meaning makers during times of loss.

Chapter Discussion

1. How can we find someone to become a compassionate listener?

2. What traits must we look for in ourselves to share another's grief journey?

Notes:

Chapter Nine: Expressing ourselves through prayer

"The need to find meaning.....is as real as the need for trust and for love, for relations with other human beings." Margaret Mead

Spirituality is the cornerstone of meaning and purpose in our lives. In the Judeo-Christian tradition spirituality gives voice to our crying out. We are familiar with our initial responses to loss. Among them are the longing, seeking and searching, anger, guilt, and feelings of abandonment. But we must always be mindful of the the resiliency factor.

Prayer and meditation can empower us in mystical ways.

Abandonment relates to our feelings of being alone and needing guidance while we are grieving. We seek meaning as is given in the psalms, prayers which offer a time- tested experience of expression.

We have noted throughout this book how we process our losses. Revising and rebuilding our lives is apparent in the psalms. They speak to our innermost concerns and needs and unlock our often hidden emotion. In psalms we are able to express our loss and the other side of sadness - our hopes.

The spirituality of logotherapy and meaning centered approaches to counseling are aided by our practice of making the psalms our own.

At one of my workshops we invited people to write a contemporary psalm, which addressed their needs. This anonymous psalm was written by a widow. She needed to find her voice and express her emotions in the genre of the psalms. The Psalms as a Judeo-Christian expression are a vehicle for creative expression and provide deep meaning.

Finding our voice

Widow's Lament

My God my spirit is weak and my body aches loneliness

consumes me as I flood my bed with tears.

Have you forgotten me O God in my plight?

Must I wait forever for strength?

Your days, O God, are timeless.

I will trust and wait for your help.

When he was with me you helped us.

In sorrows we found you.

Strengthen my weary self with your presence.

Help in these days of my life to remember your steadfast love.

This use of biblical terms and format for psalms is a personal as well as communal response to loss. There is the complaint but also the remembering that God has not abandoned her in time of sorrow. She finds her voice and purpose among others and especially with God.

Rich resources in faith, placing our loss into a meaningful context, with biblical images can help restore our lives. Biblical faith has preceded social and psychological theories. How we live is a deep concern in the scriptures. We are shown that God is not detached or uncaring. Rather God is the one who sustains us in all that we do.

The new science of bereavement is descriptive of human responses to loss. It cannot in any way take the place of religious faith. But It can serve as an instrument to describe how we find meaning according to insights and transformations people go through while they grieve.

Resilience is a key word for this developing model. Resilience describes our ability to be "wired" to go through grief. [79] But our ability to adapt to and accommodate loss must have deep origins. For the person of faith a reservoir of strength can be found in a loving God.

We seek the psalmist and the prophet to communicate wisdom about the mysteries of our lives. When we explore the scriptures we go through many changes and transformations about the meaning of the lives we live.

The creative resilient response to loss can be significantly enhanced by cultivating a biblical spirituality, a belief in something larger than ourselves, and the ephemeral nature of our existence.

Restoration

Deep reliance on God is the source for our resilience. This is not dependent on science and surveys. Rather it is an interpretive way of living our lives. God's communication to human beings is revelation, an unveiling whereby we are given ways to understand our interpretations especially about our losses.

After September 11, 2001 the American Bible Society made available a small booklet: *God Is Our Shelter And Strength, Words of Comfort and Hope from the Bible.*[80] The booklet contains scriptural quotations, which focus us on our loss and God's providential care and it has a section on how "God's makes all things New."[81]

We actually are given ways to process our losses. Recall our focus on the need to revise and rebuild our lives. In the rebuilding there is the occurrence of something new. This is a biblical way of experiencing a dual process of loss and restoration orientation while we grieve. We can read: "Watching for something new" Isaiah 43:18-21; and in the New Testament "God Will Comfort and Heal You," 2Corinthians 1.3-7.

There are intensities associated with our losses. Some loss is more intense and can be called "high Loss." Other losses may be less intense and can be called "low losses."

The degree of loss is dependent on the bond or the relationship with the loved one.

How we attribute meaning and hope to that loss makes all the difference. We do oscillate between joy and sadness as we go through grief. This is evident in the way we even converse with God about our losses.

How we go through grief is more of a philosophical/theological pursuit than a psychological journey or roadmap. Biblical reactions to loss teach us about responses which enable us to regain our equilibrium.

Jeremiah the prophet

Certain images regarding grief and mourning are significant in the scriptures. Rembrandt's painting of Jeremiah mourning after the destruction of the temple is a true biblical lament. We realize from the painting that the elements of sorrow and managing to salvage sacred vessels and the sacred scriptures is about a shattered world with still hope of restoration. The Rijksmuseum in Amsterdam gives the following description about Jeremiah:

"He had predicted the calamity. From the cave into which the prophet has withdrawn in isolation, he hardly dare look back at the battling soldiers, the burning city and the fleeing inhabitants. He has managed to save the gold vessels and the sacred scriptures from the temple. They attract attention because the light that falls on them, while the rest remains dim. That great depth too comes about through the play of light and shadow. What is more, Rembrandt knows how to evoke an atmosphere that fits well with the mood of the grieving prophet. "[84]

Rembrandt captures images from great moments in scripture in many of his paintings. They teach us about the bible and how we can experience the scriptures.[85]

The masterpiece by Rembrandt is a catalyst for meditation. It presents the prophet after the shattering of his world. He is trying to rebuild this world. So too do we do that in our lives. There are times when our world is shattered. It may be the death of a loved one, the loss of a loved one, infidelity, and the scandals to churches and our nation.

We must rebuild and our mourning, our sadness fine tunes our thoughts and emotions.

George Bonanno's words about sadness are applicable when we experience Rembrandt's Jeremiah reflection.

"People made to feel sad are more accurate in the way they view their own abilities and performance and are also more thoughtful and less biased in their perception of other people. For example, compared to angry people, sad people show greater resistance to stereotypes when they make judgments about others. In general then, sadness helps us focus and promotes deeper and more effective reflection."[86]

Lamenting

In his conversion experience St. Augustine heard children playing and singing a tune:*"Tolle Lege! Tolle Lege!"* It means to *"Take and read!"* Very often God communicates with us in extraordinary ways through ordinary experiences. It may well be the voices of children directing us toward deep meaning as it was for Augustine when he picked up the scriptures and began to read. His life was totally different from that day forward.

We need to take up and read the psalms in the Hebrew Scriptures. They give us a dimension of meaning while we grieve. They are the very prayers of Jesus in his earthly Jewish life.

At the death of a Christian the psalms have an important role in the liturgies surrounding death. The emphasis on the psalms and their use is evident in the Order of Christian Funerals:

"The psalms are rich in imagery, feeling, and symbolism. They powerfully express suffering and pain, the hope and trust of people of every age and culture. Above all the Psalms sing of faith in God, of revelation and redemption. They enable the assembly to pray in words that Jesus used during His life on earth, Jesus who knew the anguish and fear of death..."offered up prayer and entreaty, aloud and in silent tears, to one who had power to save Him out of death. Although He was Son, He learned to obey through suffering; but having been made perfect, He became for all who obey Him the source of eternal salvation. (Hebrews 5:7-9) Order of Christian Funerals.[87]"

One of the options in the Catholic funeral ritual allows for the praying of the Office. This is the prayer of the church. In the Office for the Dead we are given a way of placing our loss into the context of faith.[88]

The psalms are a source of consolation and hope while we grieve. During our time of loss we are trying with God's help to piece together broken lives. Our converse with God may well feel limited.

The psalms unlock our emotions. The words speak to us about how to process losses.

The oscillating between loss and rebuilding is a constant theme for the new science of bereavement. It is the way we cope and find meaning. The psalms in their very format in many instances allow for this. It is primarily when we pray the lamenting psalms that this is evident. These psalms relate to our "collage" of grief descriptions. (Notice once again the avoidance of grief terminology which smacks of a medicalizing of grief in describing "grief symptoms.")

In the psalms the constellation of thoughts and emotions descriptive of grief includes everything from anger, feelings of abandonment, guilt, yearning and searching as well as acceptance, trust, and new resolutions.

I recall speaking to a scripture scholar about the way the psalms were composed. He told me that they were written over time and this accounts for the change of mood. I think when we apply processing our loss to the psalms it becomes evident how they can help us revise and rebuild.

Hymns of trust

The psalms are hymns composed for a pilgrim people. They relate to our processions in life. Through poetry, prayer, and praise they lead through dark valleys to experience the restful paths of meaning.

Dietrich Bonheoffer, who was martyred during World War

II, found great solace in the Psalms. In writing from prison as he awaited execution for conspiracy in the plot to kill Hitler he wrote: *Psalms: The Prayer Book of the Bible*.

His book begins with the observation that this small book began with the observation that the Psalter is the prayer book of the Bible. He goes on to elaborate that these prayers are given by God to pray in the name of Jesus Christ.He speaks about Jesus as the one "who has brought every human sorrow and joy, every frustration and aspiration before God."[89]

The prominent scripture scholar Walter Brueggemann (1984) gives us some ways of classifying the Psalms. He divides them into three groups.

Orientation

These psalms express joy and confidence. Written in the context of well-being, they evoking gratitude for blessings.

Disorientation

These are written during times of hurt, suffering and loss. They express questions, doubts, rage and despair. Often there is confusion and a crying out.

New Orientation

These offers hope after being overwhelmed, . The petitioner of the psalm has changed and now evokes praise.

Formatting a lament psalm

We can benefit from the psalms while we grieve. They do provide the words and the very way they are composed speaks to our deepest feelings. What we have looked at in the past as a change of mood can now in light of dual processing be seen as a tool or instrument for the way we grieve. Again, we have to keep in mind the key words of "revise" and "rebuild" our world.

The following format explains not only the structure of the lament but also guidance for us in prayer.

A short cry

Usually calling upon God may be described as a short cry. While we grieve we often cry out in deep sorrow. The cry expresses human hurt. At the same time crying releases our innermost emotions.

Psalm 130

Out of the depths, I cry to you

O Lord: Lord hear my voice!

Let your ears be attentive

To my voice in supplication

Making a complaint

Praying the psalms of lament included not only the loss

of a loved one but also the other losses such as health, unjust accusations, guilt, job loss.

Complaining is spiritually healthy when we express what we feel from the very depth of our being.

Psalm 77

I pray to you Lord, God

And I beg you to listen,

In days filled with trouble,

I search for you

And at night I tirelessly

Lift my hands in prayer,

Refusing comfort

When I think of you,

I feel restless and weak.

Turning in trust

In proclaiming the psalms of lament that there is actual turning or changing from the previous focus. The crisis is resolved by our finding "renewed" meaning and trust in God.

If you, O Lord, mark iniquities,

Lord, who can stand?

But with you is forgiveness.

That you may be revered.

I trust in the Lord:

My soul trusts in his word.

Asking or petitioning for deliverance

This final format for the psalm of lament is the prayer of deliverance.

Psalm 6.4-5

In utter terror is my soul-and you, Lord, how long?

Turn, Lord, save my life; in your mercy rescue me.

The psalms give us our voice to cry out and focus on our loss. The are a necessity for our spiritual life while live and breath our sorrow and on the other side as we find joy and restoration. We must keep in mind at all times the faith of the psalmist who reminds us that: *"Unless the Lord builds the house, its builders labor in vain" (Ps. 127)*

Tool box: Keep in mind:

The psalms are a rich pastoral resource for finding, making, and expressing meaning. Our being with the bereaved is a prayerful presence. Consider which psalm you may want to pray with the bereaved.

Chapter discussion

1. How many laments (other than Psalm 23 "The Lord is My Shepherd") are we familiar with?

2. Does formatting the psalm help in our way of conversing with God?

3. Do we appreciate how the psalms help us revise and rebuild our lives?

Afterword

In many ways this book is the product of more than thirty years of being directly involved in grief ministry. The stories I hear about the old approach to bereavement continue, even as new scientific research dispels outdated ways of thinking. What has been called "good grief" is in many instances the opposite.

I fear the status quo will continue and the new way of looking at grief will not be given the significance needed.

Throughout the book I wrote about the need for a 'tool box." When we possess the right tools for caring we can do so much better. The old tools can actually do more harm than good.

We are witnessing more loss in our recent history than we ever had before as a country. We need to implement the new findings and ways of consoling others to effectively be empathic and caring human beings. Being with others is essential for good grieving. Being with the bereaved is a special calling.

Our culture is invested in commercializing and even medicalizing losses, especially death. This must stop. Conscientious religious groups with true leadership can make the difference in the American way of burial. The spiritual meaning of death cannot be overshadowed. We can no longer support the status quo.

Our thoughts, actions, and rituals must be consistent with our beliefs. We must confront the standard practices in counseling the bereaved and the methods we choose to perform the burial rites for our loved ones.

This will require a serious assessment of what we have been doing, and asking whether it simply makes sense. If the answer is obvious, we must make a commitment to evolve and do things differently. I believe we can prevail individually and as a community if we believe in the enduring human spirit.

Glossary of Terms for Bereavement

Abandonment: A feeling of being left alone, rejected, unsupported and lost. It is an emotion often felt while grieving especially with the loss of someone with whom we have had a close bond.

Acceptance: When referred to grief, this is the willing embrace of our loss.

Affectional ties: Emotional bonds of affection which vary according to our degree of intimacy or love. The severing of an affectional tie or bond can create considerable stress.

Afterlife: Refers to belief in eternal life. How one views the afterlife colors the journey through grief.

Anniversary affect: The emotions triggered by the celebration of an anniversary. This does not mean returning to square one in our grief. It is rather the confirmation that there are no time limits for our grief. It is important to celebrate the memory of loved ones at certain times. Ritual is very significant in this regard.

Anticipatory grief: The fear and sadness felt before an actual death of or separation. There is also the anticipation of releasing a loved one from suffering in the natural course of events.

Assumptive world: We mistakenly assume that our world will remain the same. The disruption of loss can create a "seismic" effect and shatter this world, which must be re-constructed.

Avoidance: This was previously thought to be an aspect of denial of grief. Now, it can be that the avoidance of acknowledging one's underlying emotional state may well be an effective way of coping with loss.

Bereavement: A stress reaction to loss necessitating our *revising* our old assumptive world and rebuilding or restoring a new world.

Burial practices: Actual ways of burial from "viewings" to internment are conditioned by our cultural framework.

Caregivers: Close family members, spouse who are attentive to the needs of the loved one, struggling with age or major illness. Beyond physical help there is the psychological pain of seeing a loved one suffer. This extends to others in professions who are with the family and sick person.

Catharsis: Crying during grief may be a cathartic experience. It is a stress reaction to loss. It is a cleansing or release of emotions when necessary for the bereaved.

Cemetery: A Place of burial for the dead. It may be consecrated or blessed ground.

Challenges: This replaces the task approach to grief. These challenges rethink the standard theories and allow the bereaved to be resilient and rebuild their worlds.

Communion of Saints: Catholic belief speaks of union with those who have died via an enduring bond. Two major feasts assert this (Feast of All Saints and Feast of All Souls).

Compassionate listener: A person who is willing to lend an empathic ear during a time of loss. This may be a trusted friend or relative who is kind, patient, and understanding. Knowledge of new approaches is really necessary for the compassionate listener to be effective.

Complicated grief: Most grief is complicated. Adjustment (not grief) counseling is required when there are deep problems in adapting to the loss. This is believed to only relate to ten to fifteen percent of the population.Most grief is normal and does not require counseling.

Constructivist theory: This theory focuses on how people give meaning to their world. It is the result of modern research and is in many ways responsible for our understanding the new science of bereavement.

Continual bonds: The maintaining of a continual relationship with the deceased. Death is not the end of a relationship. The dead person is welcomed to continue as a part of the grieving person's life. This includes the whole spectrum of past, present, and future.

Crematorium: A place where bodies are cremated for later burial. Allowed in the Catholic Church by a 1997 appendix to the *Order of Christian Funerals.(The Catholic Funeral Ritual).*

Culture: Our understanding about grief is saturated by

cultural perspective. It frames our ways of expressing our losses.

Debriefing: The World Health Organization, on its website states: "Single session psychological debriefing not recommended." The debriefing may slow down normal recovery. For the population at large it may even be counterproductive.

Debunking: Theories of grief since Freud including stage theories, phases, tasks ,rigid steps, etc. have not stood the test of modern scientific scrutiny and have been debunked by modern researchers.

Disenfranchised grief: This describes grief which is ignored or overlooked. The term was first used by Ken Doka.

Detachment: This is thought to be the end point for grief. Now the maintaining and seeing the multi-dimensional aspects of maintaining a continual bond is a healing model.

Dual processing model: This model developed to help cope with the stress of bereavement. Consists of: loss orientation-focusing on loss and the need to revise our possibly shattered world and restoration orientation focusing on rebuilding and relearning our world anew without our loved one physically present.

Enduring bond: We do not have to "let go" of our relationship with our deceased. Rather we redefine our way of maintaining a continual bond. This is a major shift in our understanding about how we grieve. The enduring bond colors our belief in eternal life.

Embalming: A peculiar practice to allow viewing of the dead body. Through a procedure using chemicals pumped into the body after death the body is preserved for the stated purpose of waking or viewing.

Equilibrium: Often our initial reactions to loss cause a psychic sense of loss of balance, which requires we regain our equilibrium. This is one characteristic of what is really a collage or grab bag of ways we react to loss. Describing grief this way is far better than to have medical language such as the "symptoms"

Forever after: Our belief in eternal life and crossing over the waters of death and entering the Reign of God. Our enduring bond of love continues in death.

Funeral industry: This is a very lucrative industry which is owned in many parts of the country by corporations. There are vault makers, casket makers, florists, special colleges in mortuary science. In many ways the American way of burial with embalming and viewings is unique. Other cultures and countries do not do what is done in the United States. Some religions do not utilize our embalming and viewing of the body after death.

Grief counseling: This is not seen as helpful when it adheres to standard models of grief. It does not allow for resilience and can place everyone into a framework of stages, phases, tasks, etc. which may do more harm than good.

Grief therapy: It is acceptable and necessary for people who are unable to cope and have other difficulties in adjusting. But it is probably only necessary for a small percentage of the population.

Grief work: Sigmund Freud gave us the phrase "the work of mourning." This influenced theories and models since 1917. They cultivated the task model of "letting go" and "reinvesting" our psychic energy. This can supposedly only be achieved by continued confrontation of memories and thoughts associated with loss. The attachment to the dead person is given up. It is the opposite to maintaining "continual bonds."

Grief outcome: The endpoint of grief not as detachment rather involves reconstruction of a relationship with the deceased.

High grief/low grief: The intensity of our grief depends on how strong or weak the ties are to the deceased. High grief usually describes a very intense love relationship (the death of a parent, spouse, sibling, or other relative that sharply differs from an acquaintance. While we may feel the loss keenly, others who do not have strong affectional ties with the deceased experience "low" grief

journaling: A creative way to give to expressing our losses. It can help discern how to dialogue with loved ones andcreate our continual bonds with them.

Laughter: A helpful quality for coping with loss. We oscillate between tears and laughter while we grieve.

Logotherapy: Originally from the Greek logos "meaning.' Victor Frankl in the concentration camp during World War II developed this on the premise that the primary motivational force of the individual is to find meaning in life.

Meaning centered counseling/therapy (MCCT): This represent meaning oriented positive psychotherapy. It utilizes the human capacity for imagination, meaning construction, responsible action, personal growth, and self regulation.

Multidisciplinary approach: This approach should be employed for better grief models. This draws from modern research methods, anthropology, sociology, psychology, philosophy, art, religion and many other sources.

Narrative/storied approach: This is a way of recounting and remembering our ongoing relationship with the deceased. From "remembering" conversations a new understanding and relationship with the deceased takes place.

New science of bereavement: New research and data gives new understanding about bereavement. It highlights resilience, seeking purpose, and enduring bonds. It is a major paradigm shift from the standard theories since 1917.

Oscillating: We sometimes focus on the pain of loss and then our minds swing to our immediate world. It is term used to describe the dynamic for dual processing our grief.

Relearning the world: When our assumptions about our world are shattered we need to relearn our world. This has been popularized by writer Thomas Attig.

Resilience: The ability to cope in better ways than we may have thought. For the most part we are "hard wired" to go through grief and regain our equilibrium.

Rites of passage: A phrase coined by French anthropologist, Arnold van Gennep. He studied rituals in the life cycle. Through ritual expression we punctuate our lives when we cross certain thresholds.

Rituals: The vehicle for expressing ourselves in word, action, and symbols. They relate to the beginning, continuation, and end of relationships. They promote our way of relating with an enduring bond of love.

Revise and rebuild: These are two key words to keep in mind especially when we want to heal and help others.

Relearning our world: The idea of relearning our world was popularized by writer Thomas Attig. He puts this forth as the central idea of grieving. It is a process of relearning our physical surroundings and relationships. It is also about relearning who we are as a person.

Remembering groups: An innovative approach for support groups. Participants explore how they live with the memories, dreams, and dialogue with their loved ones who have died. It requires new ways of thinking and relating to those who have died. It utilizes stories, rituals, and other actions to affirm the ongoing relationship with the deceased. It can be noted that those who have died are physically absent yet psychologically present.

Stages of mourning: The stage model for dying presented by Elizabeth Kubler-Ross. The assumption is that each stage is an essential component of the mourning process. This approach is now contested by many.

Stages: The stages given by Kubler-Ross had widespread usage, There were five: denial, anger, bargaining, depression, and acceptance. They were originally developed by John Bowlby.

Standard theories: The assumptions and science of the theories of grief and grief counseling are being questioned by modern research methods. Important questions as to whether these model are counterproductive are now being asked.

Storied (narrative): Recounting our story of loss through stories is a healing response to the stress of grieving. We develop and create a way of framing our losses. This is the opposite of impositions by structured theories, phases, invariant steps and stages.

Support groups: These can be a very good venue for the bereaved with support for revising and rebuilding their lives. Not a therapy group. Facilitators have to be schooled in up to date approaches and topics, which are not counterproductive. They are meant to help us relearn our world after it is shattered.

Tasks: This is the grief " work" the bereaved were to accomplish. This was invented by Dr. William Worden. It follows a mentality "that one- size- fits- all." This is now being challenged by the new science of bereavement.

Tragic optimism: Viktor Frankl maintains that meaning and hope can be found regardless of circumstances up to our last breath. It is the kind of hope that can take us through the worst storms and turmoil in life.

Bibliography

Anderson, Bernhard, W. (2000) *Out of the Depths,* Westminster John Knox Press, Louisville, London.

Arbuckle. Gerald A. (2000) *Healthcare Ministry, Re founding the Mission in Tumultuous Times,* The Liturgical Press, Collegeville, MN.

Attig, Thomas, (1996) *How We Grieve, Relearning the World*, Oxford University Press, Oxford & New York.

Attig, Thomas, (2012*), Catching Your Breath in Grief and grace will lead you home*, Breath of Life Publishing, 4-50 Dallas Rd., Canada

Augsburg, David, W. (1986) *Pastoral Counseling Across Cultures*, The Westminster   Press, Philadelphia.

Bonanno, George A., (2009) *The Other Side of Sadness, What the New Science of Bereavement* Tells us *About Life and Loss*, Basic Books, New York

Boone, Ben,(2012) *Minority Of Mind*, Syntax, 10 Becket Street, Salem, MA (Kindle Available)

Brueggemann, Walter, (2008), *The Message of the Psalms,* Augsburg Publishing, Minneapolis

Brueggemann, Walter, (1993) Praying *the Psalms*, St. Mary's Press, Winona, MN.

Campbell, Joseph, (1972*) Myths To Live By, How We Re-create Ancient Legends To Release Human Potential,* Bantam Books, New York,.

Chevaller, A. J. (1996) *On the Counselor's Path, A Guide To Teaching Brief Solution-Focused Therapy,* New Harbinger Publications, Oakland, CA.

Christensen, Michael J. and Rebecca J. Laird, (2006) Henri *Nouwen, Spiritual Direction,* Harper Collins, New York, N.Y.

Clinebell, Howard (1984) *Basic Types of Pastoral Care and Counseling: Resources For The Ministry of Healing and Growth,* Abingdon Press, Nashville

Clinebell, Howard(1979) *Growth Counseling: Hope Centered Methods of Actualizing Human Wholeness,* Abingdon, Nashville

Cole, Robert (1990) *The Spiritual Life of Children,* Houghton-Mifflin Co., Boston

Craghan, John F. (1993), *Psalms for All Seasons,* The Liturgical Press, Collegeville, MN.

Curley, Maura , (2012) *Duck in a Raincoat*, 2nd. Edition, Menukie Press/VIRGIN VOICE, Kindle (Amazon)

Curley, Terence P., (1993) *The Ministry of Consolation, A Parish Guide for Comforting the Bereaved,* Alba House, New York

Curley, Terence P. (1993) *Console One Another,* Sheed & Ward,

Kansas City, MO.

Curley, Terence P. ., (1995) *Healing The Broken-Hearted, Consoling the Grief-Stricken*, Alba House, New York.

Curley, Terence P.., (1996) *A Way of the Cross for the Bereaved,* Alba House, New York.

Curley, Terence P. (1997) *Six Steps for Managing Loss, A Catholic Guide Through Grief,* Alba House, New York.

Curley, Terence P., (2002) *Healing: Questions and Answers for Those Who Mourn,* Alba House, New York.

Curley, Terence P., (2004) *The Ministry of Consolers*, Liturgical Press, Collegeville, MN.

Curley, Terence P. ., (2005) *Planning The Catholic Funeral,* The Liturgical Press, Collegeville, MN.

Curley, Terence (2011) *Consolate il mio Popolo, Manuale per aiutare le persone in luto,* Traduzione di Luigi Dal Lago, Editrice Elledici, 10096, Leumann.Torrino, Italy

Curley, Terence P. (2011) *Peace Beyond Understanding, Consoling One Another,* Createspace.com/3492430, (Amazon.com /Kindle, Available) Marblehead, MA.01945

Del Zoppo, Patrick M. (1993) *Pastoral Bereavement Counseling A Training Program for Caregivers in Ministry to the Bereaved*, The Archdiocese of New York, N.Y.

Doka, Kenneth J. (ed.) (2002) - *Disenfranchised Grief, New Directions, Challenges, and Strategies for Practice,* Research Press, Champaign, Ill.

Doka, Kenneth J. (ed.) (2010) *Omega, Journal of Death and Dying*, Vol.61,No.4-, Baywood Publishing Co., Amityville, N.Y. pp.269-381.

Duffy, Regis A., O.F.M. (1970), *A Roman Catholic Theology of Pastoral Care*, Fortress Press, Philadelphia

Erikson, Erik H. (1950) *Childhood and Society,* W.W. Norton & Co., New York, London

Frankl, Viktor E., (1959) *Man's Search for Meaning, An Introduction To Logo Therapy*, Beacon Press, Boston, MA.

Gilbert, Richard B., (Ed) (2002) Healthcare & *Spirituality, Listening, Assessing,* Caring, Baywood Publishing Co., Inc., Amityville, New York

Gilmour, Peter, (1989) *Now And At The Hour Of Our Death*, Archdiocese of Chicago, Liturgy Training Publications, Chicago, IL.

Grimes, Ronald L. ,(ed.) (1996) *Readings in Ritual Studies*, Prentice Hall, Upper Saddle River, New Jersey.

Grollman, Earl, *Explaining Death to Children*, Beacon Press, Boston, 1967

Grollman, E., (1974) *Concerning Death : a Practical Guide for the Living* , Beacon Press, Boston, 1974

Hedtke, Lorraine, (2012) *BEREAVEMENT SUPPORT GROUPS, Breathing Life into Stories of the Dead*, Taos Institute Publications, Chagrin Falls, Ohio.

Hoff, Lee Ann, (1984) *People In Crisis: Understanding And Help-*

ing, Addison-Wesley Publishing Co., Reading, MA.

Hooyman, Nancy R. and Betty J. Kramer,(2006) *Living Through Loss, Interventions Across the Lifespan,* Columbia University press, New York.

Hutchison, Joyce and Joyce Rupp, (1999) *May I Walk You Home?,* Ave Maria Press, Notre Dame, IN.

Jewett, Claudia L., (1982) *Helping Children Cope With Separation and Loss*, Harvard Common Press, Harvard, MA.

Kalina, Kathy, (2007) *Midwife For Souls, Spiritual Care For The Dying*, Pauline Books and Media, Boston, MA.

Klass, Dennis, Phyllis R. Silverman, and Steven L. Nickman, (1996) *Continuing Bonds, New Understandings of Grief,* Taylor & Francis, Washington, D.C.

Konigsberg, Ruth Davis, (2011) *the truth about grief, The Myths Of Its Five Stages And The New Science Of Loss,* Simon & Shuster, New York.

Kubler-Ross, Elizabeth,(1969) *On Death and Dying*, MacMillan, New York

Lewis, C.S., (1961) *A Grief Observed,* Faber and Faber, London

Lilienfeld, S.O.(2007) "Psychological treatments that cause harm," *Perspectives on Psychological Science*,2,53-70.

McNiff, Shaun, (1981) The *Arts In Psychotherapy*, Charles C. Thomas Publisher, Springfield, Il.

Mitchell, Kenneth & Herbert Anderson, (1983), *All our Losses, All Our Griefs, Resources for Pastoral Care*, The Westminster

Press, Philadelphia

Mitford, Jessica, (1998) *The American Way of Death Revisited*, Vintage Press, New York.

Neimeyer, Robert A. (ed.) (2001) *Meaning Reconstruction and the Experience of Loss,* American Psychological Association, Washington, D.C.

Neimeyer, Robert A., (2006) *Lessons of Loss, A Guide to Coping*, Center for the Study of Loss and Transition, Memphis, TN.

Neimeyer, Robert A., Darcey L. Harris, Howard R. Winokuer, Gordan F. Thornton, (ed*.) Grief and Bereavement in Contemporary Society, Bridging Research and Practice,* Routledge, Taylor & Francis Group, New York, London, 2011

Neimeyer, Robert A., (2000) "Search for the meaning of meaning: Grief therapy and the process of reconstruction," *Death Studies*, 24,541-558.

Order of Christian Funerals, (1989) *International Commission on English in the Liturg*y, Liturgy Training Publications, Chicago, Il.

Poust-DeTurris, Mary (2002), *Parenting A Grieving Child,* Loyola Press, Chicago, Il.

Rogers, Fred, (1969) *Talking With Young Children About Death,* (Pamphlet) Lilly Foundation

Rando, Therese A.,(1998*) How To Go On Living When Someone You Love Dies*, Lexington Books, Lexington, MA.

Rando, Therese, A. (1984) Grief, Dying, and Death,: Clinical In-

terventions for Caregivers, Research Press, Champaign, IL.

Rando, Therese A., *Parental Loss of a Child*, (1986) Research Press, Champaign, IL.

Raphael, Beverly,(1982) *The Anatomy of Bereavement*, Basic Books, New York

Rutherford, Richard with Tony Barr, The *Death of a Christian*, *The Order of Christian Funerals*, (revised edition) 1990, Liturgical Press, Collegeville, MN.

Roberts, Darryl J., (1997) Profits *of Death, An Insider Exposes the Death Care Industries*, FIVE Star Publications, Chandler, Arizona

Rocco, Stephen R.,(2000*) Lucky To Have Me As Their Funeral Director, Interpersonal Keys to Successful Funeral Practice*, Dedham Publishing Co., Dedham, MA.

Sarnoff, Schiff, Harriet, (1996), *Support Groups, Session by Session Guide*, Penguin Books, New York.

Simsic, Wayne (1994), *Cries of the Heart, Praying Our Losses,* St. Mary's Press, Winoma, MN

Smith, Margaret, (1998) *Facing Death Together, Liturgy Training Publications*, Archdiocese of Chicago, Chicago, Il.

Stone, Howard W. (ed.) (2001) *Strategies For Brief Pastoral Counseling*, Fortress Press, Minneapolis

_____. (1987) *Crisis Counseling*, Fortress Press, Philadelphia

Stroebe M., Schut, H, *Death Studies*, (1998) Apr-May, 23(3), pp.197-224.

Switzer, David K. (2000) *Pastoral Care Emergencies*, Fortress Press, Minneapolis

Switzer, David K. (1974) *The Minister As Crisis Counselor*, Abingdon Press, Nashville,TN.

Trozzi, Maria, (1999) *Talking With Children About Loss*, Penguin Putnam, Inc., New York

Turner, Victor, (1982) *Celebration, Studies in Festivity and Ritual,* Smithsonian Institution Press, Washington, D.C.

Viorst, Judith, (1986) *Necessary Losses, The Loves, Illusions, Dependencies and Impossible Expectations That All of Us Have to Give Up in Order to Grow,* Simon & Shuster, New York.

Walter, Carolyn Amber, Judith L. M. McCoyd, (2009) *Grief and Loss Across the Lifespan, A Bio psychosocial Perspective*, Springer Publishing Company, New York

Wass, Hannelore, Robert Neimeyer, Robert,(ed.), (1995) *Dying ,Facing the Facts,* Taylor & Francis, Washington, DC.

Wicks, Robert J., Richard D. Parsons, Donald E. Capps ,(eds.) (1985) *Clinical Handbook Of Pastoral Counseling*, Paulist Press, Mahwah, New Jersey

Williams, Donna Reilly & JoAnn Sturzl, (2000) *Grief Ministry, Helping Others Mourn,* Resource Publications, CA.

Worden, J. William,(1996) *Children and Grief, When a Parent Dies*, The Guilford Press, New York, London.

Wright, H. Norman, (2003) *Crisis& Trauma Counseling, A Practical Guide for Ministers, Counselors, and Lay Counselors*, Regal

Footnotes:

[1] Tony Walter, sociologist of the University of Bath, *Time Magazine*, "Good New About Grief," Vol. 177,No.3,2011, p. 46.

[2] "MEANING MAKING IN THE DUAL PROCESS OF COPING WITH BEREAVEMENT" Margaret S. Strobe and Henk Schut chapter 3, p.63. in *Meaning Reconstruction & the Experience of Loss*, (ed.) by Robert A. Neimeyer, American Psychological Assoc. 2007

[3] "Loss and Restoration in Later Life: An Examination of Dual Process Model of Coping with Bereavement" Kate M. Bennett, Kerry Gibbons, and Suzanna Mackenzie –Smith, *Omega Journal of Death and Dying*, Vol.61, No. 5-2010 p.316.

[4] Journal of the American Psychologist cite in *The New York Times*,Feb.14,2011 (www.nytimes.com/2011/02/15/opinion/15Konigsberg.

[5] Bonanno, George, *The Other Side of Sadness: What the New Science of Bereavement Tells Us About Life After Loss,* Basic Books, New York,2009.

[6] Curley, Terence, *Console One Another A Guide for Christian Funerals*, Sheed & Ward, Kansas City, Mo. 1993

[7] American Psychological Association, Robert Niemeyer, "Constructivist Therapy Over Time," (www.apa.org/pubs/videos/4310849.aspx

[8] Thomas Attig, *Catching Your Breath in Grief...and grace will lead you home,* Breath of Life Publishing, 4-50 Dallas Rd., Canada, 2012, p.53.

[9] Bonanno, George ,A. *The Other Side of Sadness, What the New Science of Bereavement Tells Us About Life After Loss*, Basic Books, New York, 2009

[10] Thomas Attig, "Relearning The World Making And Finding Meanings," *Meaning Reconstruction & The Experience of Loss*, ed. By Robert A. Niemeyer, American Psychological Association, Washington, D.C.,2007., p.38.

[11] Hedtke, Lorraine, (2012) *BEREAVEMENT SUPPORT GROUPS, Breathing Life into Stories of the Dead*, Taos Institute Publications, Chagrin Falls, Ohio.

[12] George Bonanno., ibid. p.16-18.

[13] Ruth Davis Konigsberg, "Good News About Grief," *Time*, Vol. 177, No. 3, ,January 24, 2011., p.46.

[14] Worden, William, Grief Counseling and Grief Therapy, A Handbook for the Mental Health Practitioner, Springer Publishing, New York, Fourth Edition, 2009.

[15] Ibid.p.30

[16] Ibid.p.34

[17] Ibid. p.35 (Freud,1913,p.65)

[18] Ibid.p.37

[19] Thomas Attig, How We Grieve, Relearning the World, Oxford University Press, New York, Oxford, 1996.

[20] Ibid. p.48.

[21] Ibid. p.49.

[22] Neimeyer, Robert A. Lessons of Loss, A Guide to Coping, Center of the Study of Loss and Transition, Memphis, TN. 2006., p.40-48. (lists expanded version of challenges.)

[23] Ibid.p.41.

[24] Neimeyer, Robert, (ed.) Meaning Reconstruction & the Experience of Loss, see chapter One, "Beyond Decathexis: Toward A New Psychoanalytic Understanding And Treatment of Mourning," explains and critique's the standard model and the new approach which is "a contribution to the sea of change that is occurring in our culture's view of bereavement and mourning."

[25] Neimeyer, Robert, Lessons of Loss, A Guide to Coping, Center of the Study of Loss and Transition, Memphis, TN., 2006., p.80.

[26] Ibid.p.42.

[27] George Bonanno, ibid. p.40.

[28] Ibid. p.40.

[29] Thomas Attig, How We Grieve, Relearning the World, Oxford University Press, New York & Oxford, ,1996., vii-viii.

[30] Curley, Terence, Six Steps for Managing Loss, A Catholic Guide Through Grief, Society of St. Paul ,Alba House, New York, 1997 p.22. (This book is not about invariant steps but about finding meaning with steps based on A.A.)

[31] Lewis, C.S., A Grief Observed, Faber & Faber, London, 1961.

[32] http//keithwwatterson.wordpress.com/2011/10/07/new adaptation of CS Lewis "grief journal' strikes a cathartic chord.

[33] Ibid.p.1.

[34] Bonanno, George, ibid,p.31.

[35] Neimeyer, Robert A. (ed.) ibid. Chapter Two p. 33—53 is a detailed treatment given by Thomas Attig, "Relearning The World, Making Meaning and Finding Meaning," he gives a detailed treatment of C.S. Lewis.

[36] Neimeyer, Robert, Lessons of Loss A Guide to Coping,"p.48.

[37] Mitford, Jessica, (1998) *The American Way of* Death Revisited, Vintage Press , N.Y.

[38] Jessica Mitford, ibid.p.17

[39] Jessica Mitford, ibid. p.174.

[40] Steven Rocco, *Lucky To Have Me As Their Funeral Director, Interpersonal Keys to Successful Funeral Practice,* Dedham Publishing, Dedham, MA., 2000., p. 80

[41] *Order of Christian Funerals*, International Commission on English in the Liturgy, The Liturgical Press, Collegeville, Minnesota, 1989 The Introduction p.2-13 is essential reading to appreciate the tone the ritual wants to set.

[42] *The New Catholic Encyclopedia* (New York:McGraw-HillCo.1967,255-256.

[43] Kenneth R. Mitchell and Herbert Anderson, *All Our Losses, All Our Grief*, Resources for Pastoral Care (Philadelphia: The Westminster presss,1983),146-147.

[44] Ibid. p.146.

[45] Rutherford, Richard with Tony Barr, *The Death of as Christian: The Order of Christian Funerals*, (Revised edition), The Liturgical Press, Collegeville, MN., 1990, p.140.

[46] Peter Gilmour, *Now And At The Hour Of Our Death* (Chicago: Archdiocese of Chicago Liturgy Training Publications, 1989),13-14.

[47] Ibid..,14.

[48] Smith, Margaret, *Facing Death Together*, Archdiocese of Chicago, Liturgy Planning Publications, 1998, Chicago ,Il. P. 145.

[49] Konigsberg, Ruth Davis, *The Truth About Grief, The Myth of Its Five Stages and the New Science of Loss,* Simon & Shuster, New York, London, Toronto, Syfney,2011.

[50] Ibid. p.64.

[51] *Lessons of Loss , A Guide to Coping, ibid. p.93.*

[52] George Bonanno, Interview on Bereavement, MentalHelp.com.(This is a lengthy printed interview which covers a wide range of material on the New Science.)

[53] Ibid .Interview MentalHelp.net, March 15,2010

[54] Munch ,Edvard, These words were hand painted by Munch in poem form on the frame of the 1895 version of the painting (expressionist painter)

[55] *Man's Search for Meaning*, ibid. p.56-57.

[56] Logotherapy-Wikipedia, the free encyclopedia, http://en.wikipedia.org/wiki/logotherapy

[57] Man's search for Meaning, ibid. p.109-110.

[58] Ibid. p.68

[59] Frankl, Viktor, chapter based on lecture presented a the Third World Congress on Logotherapy, Regensburg University, West Germany, June, 1983

[60] "Basic Theoretical Concepts of Humanistic Psychology,: American Psychologist ,XXVI (April 1971),p.378

[61] Vatican Insider ,LA STAMPA, October 11, 2012.

[62] Reference Powered by Word press, http:/www.auschwitz

[63] Meaning Centered Counseling and Therapy, http://drpaulwong.com/index.php?option=com

[64] "The Defiant Power of the Human Spirit" was in fact the title of a paper presented by Long at the Third World Congress of Logotherapy in June, 1983.

[65] *The Other Side of Sadness*, ibid.p.36-43" Laughing in the Face of Death." This amplifies the importance of positive emotions from his research.

[66] Perry Biddle, "A Report: Changing Burial Customs," *The Priest*, Feb., 1996, p.19.

[67] Bonanno., ibid.,p.39.

[68] *Meaning Reconstruction & the Experience of Loss*, ibid. chapter three "Meaning Making In the Dual Process Model of Coping with Bereavement." The chapter relates to every day life experience. P.59 (schematization) and pp.55-73. You will want to spend time with this chapter.

[69] Neimeyer, Robert*, Meaning Reconstruction & the Experience of Loss*, ibid., chapter 2, Thomas Attig, p..41.

[70] *The Order of Christian Funerals*, ibid. paragraph six (par.6) refers to the "undertaker." His seems to be the preferred name for the one involve in preparation and transfer of the body.

[71] Neimeyer, Robert, Darcy C. Harris, Howard Winokuer, Gordon F. Thornton, (ed*.) Grief and Bereavement in Contemporary Society, Bridges for Research and Practice,,* Taylor & Francis Group, N.Y., London, 2011. See chapter two.

[72] *The Truth About Grief*, ibid. p.63.

[73] *Grief and Bereavement in Contemporary Society*, ibid. chapter 2 Kindle location 985of 13558%.

[74] Rando, Therese A., *Grief, Dying, And Death, Clinical Interventions for Caregivers* (Foreword by J. William Worden), Research Press Co., Champaign, Ill., p.83.

[75] Star of David Memorial Chapels website, 1236 North Wellwood Ave., West Babylon, N.Y. –information about the traditional Jewish burial customs.

[76] Wass, Hannelore, Robert A. Neimeyer, (eds*.) Dying, Facing The*

Facts, (3rd edition),Taylor & Francis, Washington, DC., ,1995 see Chapter 8, "The Contemporary Funeral: Functional or Dysfunctional" by Robert Fulton., p.193.

[77] Biddle, Perry, "A Report: Changing Burial Customs," *The Priest*, Feb., 1996, p.17.

[78] Ibid., p.19.

[79] *The Other Side of Sadness*,ibid.p.7

[80] *American Bible Society, God Is Our Shelter, Words of Comfort and Hope from the Bible*, New York, 1991-2001.,

[81] Ibid.p.25.

[82] The *Other Side of Sadness*, ibid., p.54-65.

[83] *Order of Christian Funerals*, ibid. par.71.

[84] Rembrandt,Tekst: Gerard Van Der Hoek, Rijksmuseum, Amsterdam, (guide) p. 7.

[85] Curley, Terence, *Rebuilding Trust & Hope: New Models for Grief and Mourning for the New Evangelization,* Society of St. Paul, Canfield ,Oh. Four Part Program DVD Presentation, 2012., Graphics include Rembrandt and others relating to the paradigm shift and the New Science of Bereavement.

[86] *The Other Side of Sadness*, ibid., p.31.

[87] *Order of Christian Funerals*, ibid. par.25.

[88] *Peace Beyond Understanding, Consoling One Another*, ibid. chapter 8, "The Church's Prayer for Healing and Hope", pp.111-119.

[89] Anderson, Bernhard with Steven Bishop, *Out of The Depths, The Psalms Speak For Us Today*, Westminster John Knox Press, Louisville, London, 2000 p. 3.

[90] Disenfranchised Grief-Online Grief Support.-A Social Community.com © 2012 created by Diana Young

[91] Doka, Kenneth J.,(ed*.) Disenfranchised Grief, New Directions, Challenges, and Strategies for Practic*e,
    Research Press, Champaign, Il., 2002. P.42.

[92] Kenneth Doka, ibid. p.45 "Revisiting The Concept of Disenfranchised Grief."

[93] Boone, Ben,(2012) *Minority of Mind*, Syntax Pubications,, 10 Becket St., Salem, MA. 01970. (also available on Kindle).

[94] Inside *Minority of Mind*, ibid.

[95] Ken Doka, Ibid. 188-189.

[96] *Meaning Reconstruction & The Experience of Loss*, ibid.,pp.113-134.

[97] Thomas Walsh, Rehabilitative counselor and Professor 's presentation to graduate students at St. John Seminary, Boston, MA, 2012

[98] Maura Curley, *Duck in A Raincoat*, Menukie Press VIRGIN VOICE, 2nd edition,2012, Kindle Edition,

[99] Margaret Mead, "Ritual in Social Crisis," in *Roots of Ritual*, ed. James Shaughnessy, (Grand Rapids, Mich: Ererdmans, 1973., p.89-90

[100] Turner, Victor (ed.) *Celebration Studies in Festivities and Ritual*, see "Rites of Passage::Process and Paradox," Barbara Myerhoff,pp.109-135, Smithsonian Institution Press, Washington, D.C., 1982.

[101] Van Gennep, Arnold, The Rites of Passage, translated by Monika B. Vizedom and Gabrielle L. Caffee, University of Chicago Press, 1960.

[102] Campbell ,Joseph, *Myths To Live By, How We Recreate Ancient Legends In Our Daily Lives To Release Human Potential*, Bantam Books, New York, 1972.,p.43.

[103] Curley, Terence, *The Ministry of Consolation, A Parish Guide for Comforting the Bereaved*, Society of St. Paul/ Alba House, New York, 1993., chapter 10, "Ritualizing Our Losses," p.58.

[104] Ibid. p.4-5

[105] Day of the Dead, Wikipedia the free encyclopedia PP.1-10.

[106] Wikipedia, ibid. p.3

[107] Margaret S. Stroebe, Robert O. Hansson, Henk Schut, and Wolfgang Stroebe, (2008) *Handbook of Bereavement* Research and Practice, Advances in Theory and Intervention, American Psychological Assoc., Washington, DC.. p 126.

[108] *Lessons of Loss ,A Guide to Coping*, ibid. pp. 67-77 " Ritual and Renewal"

[109] Ibid. p.69.

[110] Curley, Terence, *The Ministry of Consolers*, The Liturgical Pres, Collegeville ministry Series, 2004,p.53

[111] *Lessons of Loss, a Guide to Coping*, ibid. p.70-73.

[112] Curley, Terence, "The New Evangelization and Grief Ministry", pp.49-52, *The Priest*, November, 2012, Vol.68, No.11., pp.49-52.

[113] Terence Curley, *The Ministry of Consolers*, The Liturgical Press, Collegeville, MN., 2004, p.88-89

[114] Ibid. *The Ministry of Consolers*, chapter seven p.58

[115] Ibid. The Ministry of Consolers, chapter seven pp. 64-6

[116] Terence Curley, Six Steps for Managing Loss, Alba House, Society of St. Paul, Staten Island, N.Y., 1997.-

Other titles by Terence P. Curley

Books

Console One Another: A Guide to Christian Funerals

Consolate Il mio Popolo, Manuale per aiutare le personne in lutto

The Ministry of Consolation: A Parish Guide for Comforting the Bereaved

Healing the Broken-Hearted: Consoling the Grief-Stricken

A Way of the Cross for the Bereaved

Six Steps for Managing Loss: A Catholic Guide Through Grief

Healing: Questions and Answers for Those Who Mourn

The Ministry of Consolers

Planning The Catholic Funeral

Peace Beyond Understanding, Consoling One Another

For more information and ordering

email: manageyourloss2@gmail.com

Audio Visuals Sets

St. Paul's/ Alba House 8531 Akron-Canfield Road,
        Canfield, OH. 44406-0595

To Order: 1-800-533-2522
E-Mail : Dismas@StPAULS.US

Rebuilding Trust & Hope, New Models For Grief And Mourning For The New Evangelization

DVDAH980—4 programs, 30 minutes each (Companion DVD for this book. Produced 2012.)

Through The Dark Valley, Healing Steps for Managing Grief DVDA H821—4 programs, on a 2 hour DVD

Journey To Healing: A Ministry for the Bereaved
DVDAH370—4 programs, 30 minutes each

Arise and Walk: A Christian Grieving Guide
DVDAH880—4 programs 30 minutes each DVD

From Darkness to Light: A Healing Path Through Grief
CDAH400 2 CD's, 56 minutes each

Finding Your Way Through Grief: Spiritual Growth and Discovery During Bereavement
CDAH521—1CDO

Other Audio/Visuals - Single CDs & DVDs

For more information

Paloma Publishing

28 Allen Road, Swampscott, Massachusetts, 01907

781-592-7693

manageyourloss2@gmail.com

Journey To Healing: A Ministry for the Bereaved, (DVD)

Through The Dark Valley: Healing Steps for Managing Grief, (DVD)

From Darkness to Light, (CD)

Finding Your Way Through Grief, Spiritual Growth and Discovery During Bereavement, (CD)

Arise and Walk: A Christian Grieving Guide,(DVD)

Rebuilding Trust & Hope, New Models for Grief and Mourning for the New Evangelization, (DVD)

The Bright Promise of Immortality, New Science and Meaning for Grief Ministry (DVD)

46674704R00080

Made in the USA
Middletown, DE
30 May 2019